Adobe® Photoshop® Elements 2.0 Idea Kit

Adobe Press
Berkeley, California

Adobe Photoshop Elements 2.0 Idea Kit

Lisa Matthews

Copyright ©2003 by Lisa Matthews

This Adobe Press book is published by Peachpit Press.
For information on Adobe Press books, contact:

Peachpit Press
1249 Eighth Street
Berkeley, California 94710
510-524-2178 (tel), 510-524-2221 (fax)
http://www.peachpit.com

To report errors, please send a note to errata@peachpit.com
Peachpit Press is a division of Pearson Education
For the latest on Adobe Press books, go to
http://www.adobe.com/adobepress

Editor: Kelly Ryer
Production Coordinator: Kate Reber
Copyeditor: Judy Ziajka
Production Artist: Matt Tietjen
Indexer: Joy Dean Lee
CD Production: Victor Gavenda

ISBN 0-321-13009-X

9 8 7 6 5 4 3 2

Printed and bound in the United States of America

Contents

Introduction

The *Adobe Photoshop Elements Idea kit* delivers ideas, techniques, and templates to help you create exciting and professional-looking digital artwork using Photoshop® Elements.

Working with your own images, logos and artwork, you will learn how use Photoshop Elements to the fullest.

The accompanying CD-ROM offers templates, textures and borders. Use them with your own imagery to create printed pieces, slide presentations and Web pages.

The projects range from touching up photographs to creating newsletters, slides, postcards, posters, CD covers, ads, and Web page graphics.

To get your images ready for any of the projects you want use, follow the instructions in the Quick Fixes section: From here go to the project of your choice. All the projects contain stand-alone instructions, so just find the project suited to your needs, and get going!

Using the templates

The templates on the CD use only basic fonts available on any computers. You can choose other fonts to customize your artwork. For more font choices, visit the Adobe Web site at www.adobe.com. Adobe's Web site also has information on other Adobe software you may be interested in.

Using the projects

Each project has step-by-step instructions and design tips. Many projects also include design variations and a choice of templates to help you customize your work.

Tools:

Photoshop Elements

Materials:

Your photo

Quick Fixes: Get Your Photos Ready for Projects

Learn easy ways to fix problems such as red-eye, color imbalance, crooked images, and more

In this first project, you will learn to use some of Photoshop Elements' features to fix common image problems such as red-eye, color casts, and backlighting. Open an image that you'd like to work on. Use the techniques that are best suited to your image.

Before you start to edit your image, take a look at the following checklist to help ensure a smooth project workflow.

Create a copy of the original image. It's always a good idea to keep the original version of your photo as a backup in case you need it for any reason.

Work in RGB mode. In Photoshop Elements, you can work in RGB, Bitmap, Grayscale, or Index color mode. Very rarely will you work in any other mode than RGB. To see what mode your image is in or to change the mode, choose Image > Mode.

Restore default preferences. To make sure that all of the tools, palettes, and default values look and act like the ones in this book, you should reset the current Photoshop Elements preferences. The following directions for resetting the preferences are from the Photoshop Elements User Guide.

In Windows, press and hold Alt+Ctrl+Shift immediately after launching Photoshop Elements. Click Yes to delete the Adobe Photoshop Elements settings file.

In Mac OS, do one of the following:

• Press and hold down Option+Cmd+Shift immediately after launching Photoshop Elements. Click Yes to delete the Adobe Photoshop Elements settings file.

• Open the Preferences folder in the System Folder and drag the following files to the trash: Adobe Save For Web 2.0 Prefs and all files in the Photoshop Elements Prefs folder.

Use the correct image size

Since most projects you will work on, in this book or otherwise, call for a specific dimension, it is important to know how to set the image size.

Whether you are scanning the image yourself, using a digital camera, or simply getting your images from a Photo CD, you should know a little about image resolution.

Images in Photoshop Elements are made of pixels. Pixels are small data squares with a specific color value and location.

The *resolution* of the image refers to the number of pixels per inch (ppi). The rule of thumb is that higher resolution equals higher image quality simply because there is more information. A higher resolution also means a larger file size.

What does this mean for you? First, to check the resolution of your image, choose Image > Resize > Image Size.

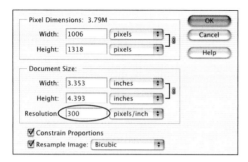

16K file size
72 x 108 pixel dim.
1" x 1.5" print size
72 ppi resolution

176K file size
200 x 300 pixel dim.
1" x 1.5" print size
200 ppi resolution

Notice that the dialog box that appears has two different sections. One gives you the actual pixel dimensions—the size the image will appear on screen—and the other gives you the document size—the resolution and print dimensions plus the file size.

72 ppi—For screen viewing of Web pages or online materials.

120 to 150 ppi—For output to typical desktop laser and ink-jet printers.

Set the resolution

You can change the resolution and print dimensions of the image by entering a higher or lower value. When you do this and the Resample Image box is checked, Photoshop Elements will either add pixels (resample up) or throw them away (downsample). Another rule of thumb: Never resample your images up. Doing so will result in poor image quality as, Photoshop Elements can only estimate what information to add; however, downsampling to make your image smaller is generally fine. Ideally, use an image with the resolution and size closest to what is needed for the final output. To get an idea of what resolutions to use, look at the following examples.

200 to 250 ppi—For most professional offset presses used for color magazines and brochures

A 72 ppi image (left) resampled up to 150 ppi (right) results in poor image quality

A 300 ppi image (left) downsampled to 150 ppi (right) results in adequate image quality

Crop and straighten your photo

Look at your image. Is it straight? Do you want to use the whole image or just a section? There are several ways to crop and straighten your image. The one you choose will depend on how much you want to crop.

Trim and straighten your photo.
If your image is crooked because of a sloppy scan, the easiest way to fix it is to choose Image > Rotate > Straighten and Crop Image. Elements will automatically crop and straighten it for you.

Perhaps your image is crooked because of a bad camera angle, or maybe you just want to get rid of an insignificant element in the outer corner. Select the Crop tool (⛏) from the toolbox. Then click and drag around the area of the image that you want to keep. Once the area is selected, you can perform any of the following actions:

• Drag a corner or edge to resize the area of the crop.

• Place the cursor over a corner handle and drag in the direction you want to rotate.

• Place the cursor inside the bounding box and drag to reposition it.

When trying to straighten your image, find a true 90-degree angle to use to align your cropping tool. Pillars and picture frames work well, for example

When you are finished, press Enter to complete the crop. If you change your mind, Press Esc to cancel.

Variation: Crop to an exact dimension and resolution

You may occasionally need to crop to an exact dimension and resolution. For example, you may need a head shot that is 1 inch by 1 inch and 150 dpi. To achieve this, select the Crop tool. Notice that the options bar now gives you a place to enter height, width, and resolution. Enter your values. Now when you drag the cropping tool, it will allow only those dimensions.

Make sure that the image resolution is higher than or equal to the one to which you are cropping to avoid resampling up.

Fix red-eye

The common problem of red-eye is now easily fixed using the Red Eye Brush tool (🖌).

Zoom in. It's always a good idea to zoom in on the area you want to edit so you can see the details. Choose the Zoom tool (🔍) from the toolbox. Drag around the area you want to work on.

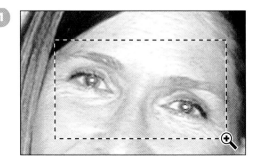

Set up the Red Eye Brush tool. Select the Red Eye Brush Tool and position it over the color you want to replace. Hold down the Alt/Option key. The Eyedropper tool appears. Click the red area of the eye to sample that color. The color will appear on the options bar under Current Color. This tells Photoshop Elements to paint over only that particular color and ones similar to it. You can control which colors Elements considers similar by adjusting the Tolerance slider located on the options bar. If you don't get the color you want, you can easily change it by sampling again.

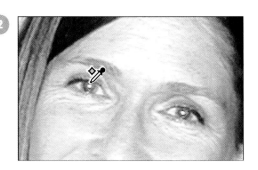

When you have the color set, click the Replacement Color palette. In the color picker, move the circle until you find a color that you want to use.

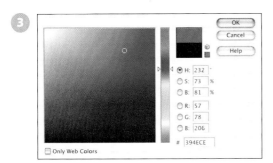

Select a brush. Choose your brush size using the slider on the options bar. The default setting is 7. Depending on the resolution of your image, you may find it easier to work with a slightly larger or smaller brush. Finally, paint over the area until you are satisfied with the results.

Correct for backlighting. Often you may take a picture where the foreground is dark and the background is perfectly exposed. The subject could be in front of a window, a sunset, or some other light source. The ideal way to avoid this problem is use an on-camera flash. Nevertheless, some of your photos will have backlighting problems. Fortunately, Photoshop Elements provides a feature called Fill Flash that easily remedies the problem.

To use the Fill Flash feature, choose Enhance > Adjust Lighting > Fill Flash. Make sure that the Preview box is checked; then use the sliders to adjust the lightness and saturation until you are satisfied with the results.

Use fill flash

Enhance your colors

Sometimes your photo may have an un-natural color tint. Fluorescent lighting, tungsten lights, and bad scans are just a few of the potential culprits.

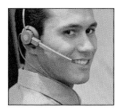 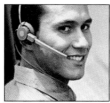

Fluorescent light may cause a green cast. Add magenta to balance.

Tungsten lights may cause a yellow cast. Add blue to balance.

Correct color casts. To adjust the color in your image, select Enhance > Adjust Color > Color Variations.

Select Midtones. The midtones are colors that are not in a shadow or highlight and often contain the dominant color cast. If you have color cast that does appear in the shadows or in the highlights of your image, you can adjust it as well. Select the color you want to add or subtract from the examples below. You can compare your original image in the upper left corner to the color-corrected image on the right.

To adjust the amount of color saturation (color purity) in your image, select Saturation and make adjustments as you did for Midtones.

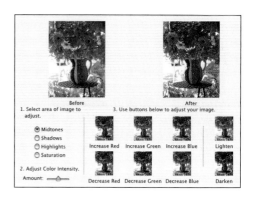

Sharpen the photo

Many photos can use a little sharp-ening. The Unsharp Mask filter works great to sharpen image details. If you have adjusted the resolution of your image, it is best to make this the final step of your photo correction.

1 **Set the zoom percentage to 100%.** Double-click the Zoom tool ( ) to set the photo to 100% magnification.

Sharpen the image. Choose Filter >
Sharpen > Unsharp Mask. Select the
Amount slider and drag until you see a
positive result. To preview a specific
part of the image, place the cursor in
the regular image and move it to the
specific area of interest (the cursor will
turn into a box). You might want
to look closely at hair, eyes, and foliage,
where sharpening can be dramatic.
It's easy to apply this tool to fix blurry
pictures, but oversharpening can also
leave your image with a distracting
grainy texture.

Save the file

If you are happy with the final results of
your image, choose File > Save As,
rename the file, and save it in
Photoshop format.

Ever wonder how to get those great photos that pop off the page? The following tips will give you some ideas you can try the next time you're out with your camera and will help you spend less time in Photoshop Elements doing fix-up.

ACTION!

Try to anticipate the exact moment. Shoot extra frames before and after. If your camera has a continuous shooting mode, this is the place to use it.

DIFFERENT PERSPECTIVE

Try shooting from different angles and points of view.

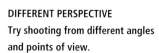

DYNAMIC

To help focus all of the attention on your subject, shoot against a plain or neutral background. If your focus is the big picture, include more of the surrounding elements.

Project 1

Make Your Subject Stand Out

Put your subject in a whole new setting by manipulating the background or changing it altogether.

A fun and easy way to make sure that your subject is the focal point of your photo is to use Photoshop Elements Selection Brush tool. This tool allows you to select and separate your subject from the background so you can edit it or change it completely.

1 Get started. Open the image you want to edit in Photoshop Elements.

2 Zoom in on your subject. Using the Zoom tool (🔍), click an edge of the foreground subject.

3 Set masking options. With the Selection Brush tool you create your selections by painting the area you want to select either in Selection mode or Mask mode. In Mask mode, the Selection Brush tool selects the inverse of what you are selecting while giving you a colored preview of the mask you are creating over your subject.

Once you have zoomed in on your subject, select the Selection Brush tool (🖌). On the options bar, select the Mask mode. Set the opacity to 50 percent. You can also change the color or leave it set to the default red.

This will allow you to see the selection mask you are creating over your subject more clearly.

4 Choose your brush. Now that you have set your mask options, you want to do the same for your brush.

Click the Brushes pop-up menu. As you can see by scrolling through the list, there are many options. Start with a medium-size soft brush.

5

Select your edges. To make your life easier, first set the edge boundaries and then move inward. Start by painting around the edges of your subject. We are using a soft brush to avoid the harsh cut-out look. A softer selection around your subject allows you to blend your final background in a more natural fashion. If you accidently paint where you don't want to, switch to Selection mode on the options bar and paint over the area.

6

Photoshop Elements' Selection Brush Mask mode allows you to easily select odd-shaped areas in your image. If you are in Mask mode, a temporary colored overlay appears over the unselected areas and exposes the selected areas of the image. When you toggle back to Selection mode, you will see the "marching ants" marquee around the selection you made.

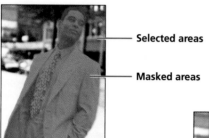

— Selected areas

— Masked areas

Painting with the Selection Brush in Mask mode gives you a colored preview of the area you are masking out.

When you toggle back to Selection mode, you will see the resulting selection.

Complete the mask. Once you've finished selecting the edge of your subject, select a larger, hard-edged brush from the Brushes menu. Paint freely inside your new edge until your subject is covered.

Select your subject. Toggle back to the Selection mode. You should see the selection marquee around your subject and background edges. The background area around your subject is now selected. To isolate your subject within its own selection, choose Select > Inverse. This reverses your selection.

Create a new layer. Choose Layer > New > Layer Via Copy. This will place a copy of just your subject on a new layer. If your Layers palette is not visible, choose Window > Layers or click the Layers tab in the palette well. The Layers palette shows two separate layers: one for the background and another above it that should contain a copy of your subject.

Alter the background. On the Layers palette, click the Background layer to select it. Choose Filter > Blur > Gaussian Blur. Drag the slider until you get an effect you are happy with. Because you have selected only the Background layer, your subject will not be affected. If you are not happy with the results, or if you want to try another filter, choose Edit > Step Backward or Ctrl/Cmd+Z.

10 **Save a working version of your photograph.** It's always smart to save a layered working version of your file in case you want to make changes down the road. To save your new version with layers, choose File > Save As, rename the file, and save it in Photoshop format. If you want to save a single-layer version (commonly known as flattened version), choose File > Save As, rename the file, and deselect the Layers check box. The Save a Copy check box will automatically be selected. Rename your file and save it.

Variation: Experiment with filters

Background with Diffuse Glow filter   **Background with Radial Blur filter**

Photoshop Elements has lots of filters and interesting effects. Now that you have your background on a separate layer, you can experiment with them. To see examples of all of the filters, choose the Filters tab. When you see a filter you want to try, select it and click Apply.

Variation: Adjust the color of the background

Sometimes it can really be effective to change or remove the color of the background. To do this, choose Image > Enhance > Adjust Color. Then you can choose Hue/Saturation, Replace Color, Remove Color, or Color Variations.

Variation: Use a different image for the background

By now, you are probably realizing that your choices are fairly limitless. You may even be wondering how to go about placing your subject on a whole new background.

①

Add a new background image. Open the photo or image that will be used for the new background. (Make sure that your working file is still open and that the Background layer is selected.) Place the two image windows side by side. With your new image active, select the Move tool (⯈⊹) from the toolbox. Click the image and drag the new background into your original working file.

②

Position the new background. Select your working file. On the Layers palette, select your new background layer. Use the Move tool to move it to a position that works with your subject. Save your file.

Project 2

Hand-Color Your Photographs

Use the painting tools in Photoshop Elements to change or add colors in your photographs.

In this project, you learn to remove color from your photograph and replace it using the painting features. We're using a couch, but this is a technique you can try on people, scenery, cars—you name it!

Note: If you are working on a black-and-white image, you'll need to change the image mode to one that allows colors. Choose Image > Mode > RGB Color. This will allow you to colorize the image.

Get started. Open your image in Photoshop Elements.

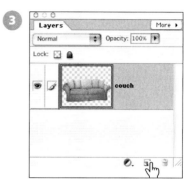

Create a new layer. If the Layers palette is not visible, click the Layers tab in the palette well or choose Windows > Layers. Click the New Layers button (⬚) at the bottom of the palette.

Remove the current colors. Unless the image you are using is already a black-and-white image, you will want to remove the colors. Choose Enhance > Adjust Color > Remove Color.

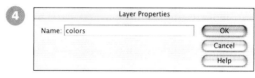

Set layer options. You should always give your layers a descriptive name. This way, even if your file has 50 layers, you can easily identify the one you want. Double-click the new layer to bring up the Layer Properties box. Type Colors as the layer name.

Next, you will set the layer blending mode. The blending modes are located on the pop-up menu next to the opacity settings on the Layers palette. Click the menu and select Color. This setting will allow the image to show through the color.

5 **Pick your paint brush.** Select the Paintbrush tool (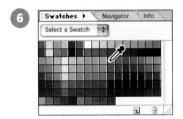) from the toolbox. From the Brushes pop-up menu on the options bar, select a medium-size brush for painting. The brush settings appear on the options bar after you select a brush. Note: The brush size will also depend on the resolution of your image. A medium-size brush for a 300-dpi image will be a large brush for a 72-dpi image.

6

Choose your paint color. At the bottom of the toolbox, click the Set Foreground Color swatch (■). Use the vertical sliders to find the color area you desire. After you have that set, use the circle to select the exact color you want. Alternatively, choose Window > Color Swatches and click the color you want. You should see the color you've selected in the Foreground color swatch.

7

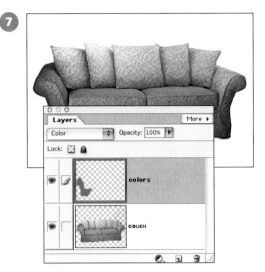

Begin painting. Select your new layer. Zoom in on the area you want to paint. Drag your paintbrush over the area to apply the new color. If you find that your brush is too large, too small, or wrong in some other way, go back to the Brushes menu and select a new brush.

8 **Make corrections.** It happens to the best of us: we make a mistake or change our minds. There are three ways to deal with this. If you just applied the action, press Ctrl/Cmd/+Z. If you want to undo more than one step, go to the Undo History palette. This nifty palette allows you to go back 20 steps! The final option to correct a mistake is to use the Eraser tool. The Eraser tool has three forms: Eraser, Background Eraser, and Magic Eraser. Here, just choose the plain Eraser tool. After you have chosen the eraser mode, you can choose Brush, Pencil, or Block. Choose a setting to complement your current paintbrush and drag over the offending area.

Experiment with color. To add more colors, just go back to step 6 and choose a new color.

Create new layers for your new colors and experiment with different layer modes and paintbrushes.

Save a working version. To save your new version with layers, choose File > Save As, rename the file, and save the file in Photoshop format. If you want to save a single-layer (flattened) version, choose File > Save As, rename the file, and deselect the Layers check box. The Save a Copy check box will automatically be selected. Rename your file and save it.

Variation: Create an old-style sepia-tone photograph

Use this variation to give modern-day images that old-time feel.

Set colors. Follow step 2 to desaturate your image. Set your color swatches to their default black and white by clicking the Default Colors icon (■). This sets the foreground color to black and the background color to white.

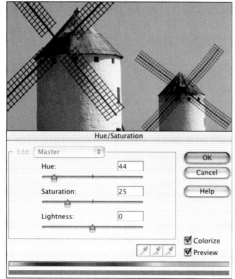

Go back in time. For this color effect, we are going to use a nondestructive adjustment layer. The marvelous thing about adjustment layers is that you can always go back and change them or delete them. To create an adjustment layer, choose Layer > New > Adjustment Layer. For this example, choose Hue/Saturation for Type. In the Hue/Saturation dialog box, select Colorize. Drag the Hue and Saturation sliders to achieve a brownish tone.

Experiment with different painting techniques and come up with your own look.

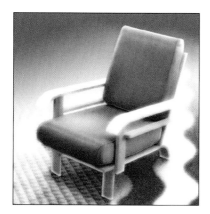

BREAK OUT!
Color outside the lines. Use a large, soft brush for a glowing effect.

CREATE A PALETTE
Make your own palette of colors that work well with each other.

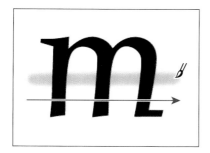

HIGHLIGHTS
Create a highlight by hand-painting one object in your image.

MODES MODES MODES
If you decide to paint with different colors on the same layer, set the blending mode to Behind on the Paintbrush Options palette. This will keep the different colors from interfering with one another.

Project 3

Create Multiple Photo Pages

Duplicate your image in multiple sizes for print.

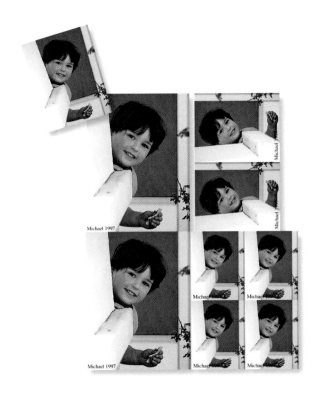

Have you ever had an image that you wanted to make into a holiday card or duplicate for friends and relatives? Here is a super-easy way to create a multiple-picture layout using just one file.

① **Edit your image.** Make all of the necessary edits to the image you want to use. Since you will be printing it, the resolution should be between 150 dpi and 300 dpi depending on how big you want the prints to be. Save a copy of the file. You can also leave the file open if you want.

② **Choose your file.** Choose File > Print Layouts > Picture Package. Under Source, do one of the following;

• If your image is still active, select Use Frontmost Document.

• If the image is not still active, navigate to your file on the hard drive and select it.

③

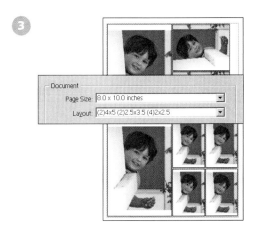

Set layout options. Under Layout, choose a template that will suit your need. Note: Use the online help system in Photoshop Elements if you want to create a new template or edit an existing one.

④

Set the resolution. Enter the final resolution you want for your printed image. If you are uncertain what resolution to choose, enter 150. Remember that the higher the resolution (dpi), the sharper the image, and the bigger the file size.

Select RBG if your image is in color, and Grayscale if it is in black and white.

Go. Click OK to create your picture package. When it is done, save the file. Your image is now ready to print!

Variation: Add text automatically

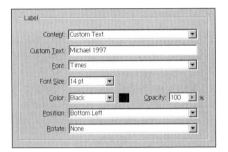

Enter the text. Suppose you want
to add a label with the name of your
subject and the date that the photo
was taken. You can do this in
Photoshop Elements using the text
tool, but there is an easier way. Go to
the Label area located at the bottom of
the Picture Package dialog box. In the
Custom Text field, enter your text.
Proceed through the remaining boxes
to customize the font, size, color, and
position of the label.

Tools:

Photoshop Elements

(Optional) PageMaker

Materials:

Your Photos

Templates

Project 4

Create a Contact Sheet for Your Image CD

Easily create thumbnails of all of your images by creating a contact sheet that will fit into any jewel case.

How often have you burned a CD of all of your images but then wanted a quick way to reference them at a glance? The automated contact sheet feature in Photoshop Elements gives you an easy way to do this.

1 **Get started.** Create a folder on your desktop. Place all of the images that you want on the contact sheet in that folder.

2 **Choose your source.** Choose File > Print Layouts > Contact Sheet. Under Source, click Choose and navigate to the folder you created in step 1.

3

Set up your file. Under Document, type 4.75 for Width and Height. Make sure that the measurement units are set to inches.

For Resolution, type 150 or 300. Even though your images will be quite small, you want to be able to see them clearly. A higher resolution will help.

Choose RGB Color for Mode. If your images are black and white, then choose Grayscale.

4
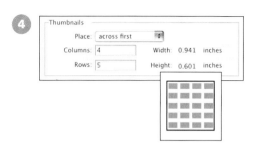

Image layout options. Under Thumbnails, you can specify the number of images that appear on a page and how they are sorted. Click Place and choose Across First or Down First. The Columns and Rows settings determine the size of the thumbnails. Experiment to figure out what works best for you. Your settings will depend on whether your images are horizontal, vertical, square, or rectangular.

5

Create the reference label. If it is not already checked, select Use Filename as Caption. Photoshop Elements will then label the image with its existing name. Choose a different font and type size if you want. Click OK. Photoshop Elements will then begin placing all of your images into one file. If you have more than will fit on a page, it creates a new file. When the images are all in the file, save and then print your new contact sheet.

Variation: Create a title

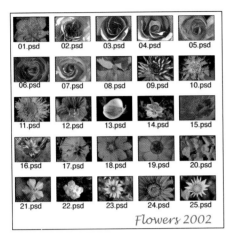

Add a title in Photoshop Elements using the Type tool. After Elements has created the contact sheets, there is more you can do. For instance, you might want to title your CD.

To do this, select the Type tool from the toolbox and click the image. This is where you will enter your text. You can always move the text later though, so don't worry if it's not exactly where you want it.

After choosing the font and size, enter your text for the title. When you have finished, use the Move tool (⌖) to move the title into place.

Once you have your contact sheets, you can go a step further. Using the PageMaker templates provided with this project, you can create an actual double-sided booklet that contains your contact sheets and any other information you want to add. The templates are located on the CD in Project folder number 4.

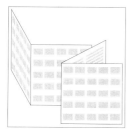

FOLD IT!
This is an example of a folding CD cover.

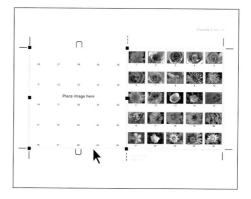

IMPORT YOUR IMAGE
After you have edited the text, place your images. Select the placeholder frame at the right of the first page and choose File > Place. Navigate to your first contact sheet and click Yes. This is now the front cover of your booklet.

Repeat this step if you have more than one contact sheet to place.

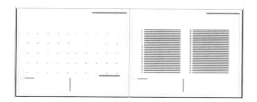

USE THE TEMPLATE
Use PageMaker 7.0 to open the template provided with this project. After you open it, save it with a new name. Notice the placeholders for text and images. To alter the text, select the Type tool, then highlight the template text and enter your own in place of it. If there are unneeded text blocks, simply delete them.

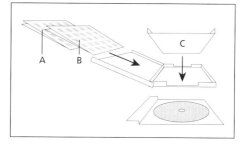

SAVE, PRINT, AND ASSEMBLE
After you have finished creating your layout, save the file; then print and assemble the CD case according the diagram above.

Project 5

Create a Panoramic Image

Let Photoshop Elements automatically create your panoramic image or do it yourself.

This technique is for all those fabulous scenes where your camera lens wasn't quite wide enough. You can use it for long, wide landscapes or even for piecing together the façade of a grand building.

Organize your images. Once you have all of the images you want to combine, place them in one folder for easy access.

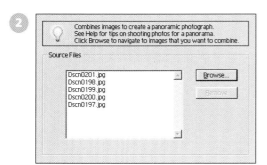

Choose your files. Open Photoshop Elements and choose File > Create Photomerge. Under Source, click Browse and navigate to your folder of images. Select the first image and click Open. You can also select a group of images by holding down the Shift key as you select.

Merge your images automatically. After you have selected all of your files, click OK. Photoshop Elements will then begin to auto-match your images together. When it is finished, you should see the combined images in the Photomerge dialog box, as in the example above.

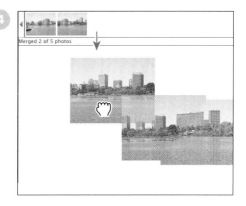

Merge your image manually. Often, Photoshop Elements is unable to place all of your images automatically. When this happens, it will place your images in the thumbnail box above the arranging area. To manually arrange your images, choose the Select Image tool from the toolbox and then drag the thumbnail into the arranging area.

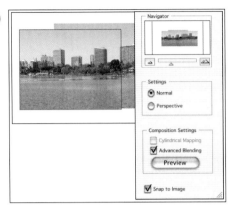

Set up your options. When your image is selected in the arranging area, you will see a red highlight around it. In the dialog box at the right are all of the options for merging your images together.

To get things started, you may want to turn on Snap to Image. Next, click Perspective to set the vanishing point. Select the Vanishing Point tool from the toolbox and click the image where the vanishing point should be. You will see the images adjust to that perspective. Note: Depending on how your images were shot, you may want to use the Rotate Image tool as well.

Finally, to eliminate any differences in exposure, choose Advanced Blending and click preview. You may still need to do some touch-up in the final file. If you are happy with the result, click OK. Elements will then create a new file with your combined image.

Edit your new file. Okay; you have your new panoramic image, but it still looks a little less than perfect. Use the Crop tool to edit out the ragged edges, and make any other edits the image may need such as adjustments to the color, lighting, and other properties. Choose File > Save As and save your panoramic image with a new name.

Variation: Merging other images

The Photomerge feature doesn't have to be used to create horizontal panoramas. For instance, on your trip through Italy, you may find all sorts of grand church façades, but suppose your camera lens isn't wide enough to capture them? Shoot each part of the façade and then piece it back together using Photomerge.

Once you're done merging the image, click OK to create the new file. Crop and edit the file as needed. Choose File > Save As and save the merged image with a new name.

You may be wondering if there are any good tricks for creating a panorama or other type of merged image. Take a look at the examples here for some tips on how to create seamless, natural-looking merged imagery.

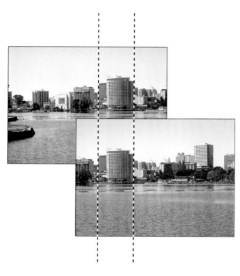

EXPOSURE

Keep the exposure as consistent as possible. This will help you avoid spending time performing lighting and color edits in Photoshop Elements.

RULE OF THIRDS

It's best if your images can overlap by a third (or more). This gives you something to match up.

DON'T MOVE!

Seriously, when you are shooting images that you plan to merge, stay in the same place. This is an instance where you want to, at the very least, keep the same height and perspective. Obviously, if you are shooting architecture, this can't always be done. Just remember: the more angle changes you make, the more finessing you'll need to do with the Perspective tool.

Project 6

Accent Your Photograph with a Border

Add a finishing touch to your image by using a border.

Placing a border around your photograph is one of the best ways to add a finishing touch. You can either use one of the premade borders shown in the example on the right or create your own by following the instructions.

1 Get started. Open the photograph or image you want to use in Photoshop Elements.

2 Size your photograph. Using the Crop tool, crop your photograph to 3 inches by 3 inches with a resolution of 200 pixels per inch (see "Use the correct image size" on page 3 for instructions).

After your photograph is resized, you can use any of the borders provided in the project.

3 Select your border. Look through the border templates in the Print folder inside the Proj06 folder. You can also choose one by looking at the examples. Open the template you want to use. Note: Templates P06a.psd through P06d.psd are geared for images that will eventually be placed against a colored background.

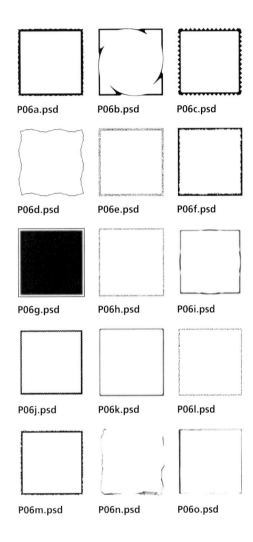

P06a.psd   P06b.psd   P06c.psd

P06d.psd   P06e.psd   P06f.psd

P06g.psd   P06h.psd   P06i.psd

P06j.psd   P06k.psd   P06l.psd

P06m.psd   P06n.psd   P06o.psd

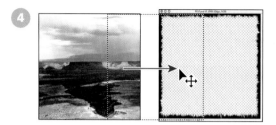

Place your image within the border.
Make sure that both your photograph
file and border file are open. Place the
image windows side by side, to make
them easily accessible. Click your
photo window to make it active.

Select the Move tool (▶+) and place the
cursor in your image. Hold down the
Shift key and drag your photo onto the
border image. You can release the
mouse after you see the move highlight
over the border window. You have just
copied your image within the border.

Holding down the Shift key while you
drag forces Photoshop Elements to
center your photograph within the
border window. If you didn't hold
down the Shift key, you can always
reposition the image by using the Move
tool again.

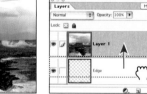

Arranging your layers. You cannot
see your border at this point. This is
because you still need to reposition the
layers. Start by clicking the border

window to make it active. To see your
layers, click the Layers tab in the
palette well at the top of the screen.
There will be two layers: the border
layer (at the bottom) and your image
layer (on top). To reposition the layers,
do one of the following on the Layers
palette:

• Drag the border layer above the
image layer.

• Drag the image layer below the
border layer.

You will now see the border around
your photograph.

Save a copy of your file. Save a copy
of your file with the new layers. Choose
File > Save As, rename the file, and
save the file in Photoshop format. If
you want to save a single-layer
(flattened) version, choose File > Save
As, rename the file, and deselect the
Layers check box. The Save a Copy
check box is automatically selected.
Rename your file and save it.

Variation: Change the border dimensions

What happens if your image doesn't
fit within the border dimensions?
No problem; you can still use the
borders with a little adjustment.

Simply open the border you want to use and choose Image > Image Size and set the height and width to values matching your image. You can then continue with step 4 to copy your photo into the border window.

Variation: Images destined for the Web

You may be planning on posting your finished images on the Web. If so, you have a couple of options.

Use for Web. The Save for Web option is the easiest approach if you want to keep a higher-resolution file on hand for printing, but you also want a low-resolution version for the Web. Once you have completed steps 1 through 6, keep the file open and choose File > Save for Web.

In the Save for Web dialog box, enter new size values under New Size. Click Apply.

Next, go to Settings, located above Image Size. If you are using templates P06a_w through P06d_w, then choose GIF and click the Transparency check box. If you are using any other

template, you can choose either GIF or JPEG, depending on what works best with your image.

Note: You can also see how big your file is going to be below the image preview.

When you are satisfied with your settings, click OK and save.

Use a template specified for the Web.

If your images are going to be used on the Web only, you may want to use a template set up for the Web. In step 2, set the resolution to 72 pixels per inch. Open a template of your choice located in the Web folder of Project 6 and proceed with steps 3 through 6 of this project.

Variation: Change the borders

Just because you are using a template doesn't mean that you can't give it your own style. One way is to apply some color. This variation works best with templates P06a.psd through P06d.psd, P06f.psd, and P06g.psd (in either the Print or Web folder).

Set up your target layer. After you have rearranged the layers in step 5, select the border layer on the Layers palette and select the Preserve Transparency box on the Layers palette. This will allow you to edit the border without affecting the rest of the layer.

Give the template some color. Choose the color you want to use. Then choose Edit > Fill. Under Contents, choose Foreground Color. Click OK to fill the border with the new color.

Variation: Create your own!

Flex your creativity: Try your hand at creating your own border. One advantage of this approach is that you can add a border without having to resize or crop your original photo.

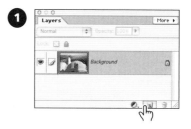

Create a new layer. Open your photo as in step 1 of the project. Click the Layers tab to bring up the Layers palette. Then click the New Layer button at the bottom of the palette to add a new layer to your photo.

Set your border. Click the new layer and choose Select > All or press Ctrl/Cmd+A. This selects the entire layer. Now you need to define the border area. Select the Rectangular Marquee tool (⬚). Hold down the Alt/Option key and drag in the interior area of the photo that you want framed by the border. Note: You can use the Elliptical Marquee tool as well. To reposition the selection as you draw, press the spacebar and drag with the Alt/Option key still pressed.

When you hold down the Alt/Option key, the selection is subtracted from the interior area, leaving just the border area selected.

Fill the selection. Choose a color and then choose Edit > Fill. Under Contents, choose Foreground Color. Alternately, select the Paint Bucket tool and click the selected area.

Border created using Angled Strokes and the Fragment filters.

Experiment! Photoshop Elements ships with all sorts of filters. Click the Filters tab to see examples of them. When you see one you want to try, double-click it to apply it to your layer.

A little border can go a long way. Try to avoid borders that are so overly colorful, large, or complex that they become more gaudy than decorative. They detract from the image or message that you are trying to achieve. Here are a couple of tips to keep in mind when creating borders.

When you create your border, remember that the attention is supposed to be on the image, not the border. Make sure that the size and colors are appropriate for the image.

If you will be placing the photo in a some sort of publication, you don't need to add a keyline around the photo. Your image has a stylized border already, so you don't need to add another one.

SYTLES

Choose a border style that matches your subject matter. For example, ornate borders can often be used with images of historical or traditional content, while a contemporary border like the Polaroid transfer look of P06b.psd can work with an offbeat image.

Tools:

Photoshop Elements
PageMaker (Optional)

Materials:

Newsletter template
Your photos

Project 7

Publish Your Photographs in a Newsletter

Get your color photos ready for black-and-white or one-color reproduction.

ZZZinsider

THE SLEEP INDUSTRY SPECIALISTS   *Spring Edition*

NEW FACES

Liz Budo appointed to Board of Directors

This Quarter

New appointment to Board of Directors.

Product line expands to include featherbeds.

Company picnic planned for August on Farallon Islands.

Write to us at editor@zzz.com.

The stock price soared last month in response to the anticipated appointment of Liz Budo to the Board of Directors of ZZZ company. Liz joined ZZZ last November as Senior Vice President for Corporate Development. She flew in to the Detroit office just long enough to accept the appointment **before she was whisked away to** Headquarters to meet with the Chairman of the Board.

Liz most recently worked at Snore, Inc. in Minneapolis, where she was head of the product development. One of her more notable accomplishments at Snore was to establish a venture capital fund to foster development of new technology in the industry. **When Liz started the Fund in 1990,** she based it on a philosophy that con **tinues to guide Snore, Inc. in manag-** ing their fund today: Deliver consis **tent performance with limited risk.** That firm belief helped the Snore fund to succeed.

Company picnic planned for August

If you've just recently joined the **staff at ZZZ Company, you may** not have heard yet about our company picnics.

Some company picnics have given the word "picnic" a bad name. They make you think of going to the same park every summer, drinking a beer, eating some potato salad and a hot dog, and standing around, trying to **think of something to say to** your fellow employees. You **stand around for awhile, maybe walk over and watch the raffle going on at the stage nearby, say** "Hi" to a couple of employees and try to remember their

Bob takes the Surfing trophy

names, eat some dessert, and **then you go home. Sound like fun? Well, if this is what you're** expecting to sign up for at the summer picnic this August, you'll be disappointed.

To give you an idea of what ZZZ company picnics are like, let's talk about the last few picnics. Ask John Peppersmith to tell you about the sunburn he got while sailing to the myster **ous island somewhere in the** Pacific. Ask Regimond Donald son how he got that scratch on **his leg while hiking through** prickly brambles to the secluded waterfall. And ask Marylu Tall feather about the giant fossil egg that's **displayed on her desk. But don't** worry. They still got **to eat hot dogs and drink beer.**

Let's say you're putting together a short newsletter for work, school, or a holiday family update. More than likely, it will be printed in black and white. This project gives you the steps to get your image ready.

When you are done editing your image, you can place it in the page layout program of your choice. We've included a newsletter template that you can use if you have a copy of Adobe Pagemaker 7.0, but it's not required for this project.

①

Get started. You should decide what photos you want to use and what the final printed size will be. Check the resolution of your images. The resolution should be at least 300 pixels per inch (see "Use the correct image size" on page 3).

②

Open your photo. Open your first photograph in Photoshop Elements. Take a hard look at it. Are there distractions that could be taken out? Do you want to zoom in on just one person?

③

Trim and size the image. Select the Crop tool to trim your image to the correct dimensions. Use the options bar to set the exact image size. If the entire image needs to be smaller, choose Image > Image Size and enter the dimensions (see "Use the correct image size" on page 3).

If you are going to use the optional PageMaker template, use the following image dimensions for the front page: 2.65 inches wide by 2.65 inches high for the first image, and 1.69 inches wide by 1.69 inches high for the second image.

Remove the color. To convert your image to grayscale, choose Image > Mode > Grayscale and click OK. (Remember that it's always a good idea to save a backup version in color before converting your image.)

Adjust the contrast and sharpen. You may notice a loss of contrast and tonal range when converting from color to grayscale. If this is the case, choose Enhance > Adjust Brightness/Contrast > Levels. Drag the triangular sliders under Input Levels to adjust the tonal range. Make sure the Preview box is checked so you can see what is happening to your image. (For more information on levels, refer to the online Photoshop Elements user guide.)

Finally, to make your image a little snappier, choose Filter > Sharpen > Unsharp Mask. Drag the Amount slider until you are satisfied with the result. Remember to look at detailed areas such as hair, eyes, and foliage. These areas will often benefit from sharpening. Also remember that too much sharpening is not good for smooth areas such as skin tones or blue skies, which tend to become grainy.

Save in TIFF format. One of the widely used printing formats is TIFF. To save your document as a TIFF file, choose File > Save As and save your changes in TIFF format. Make sure you also save the original version as well.

You are now ready to place your image in PageMaker or any other layout software. To use the provided template, open PageMaker and then open template P07.t7, located in the Project 7 folder.

Variation: Add a little color

Here is a great technique if you are printing on a personal color printer and want an image with a certain hue: for example, if you are going to print a head shot, and you want it have a warm sepia tone.

Note: If you are using a professional printer and want to add a color, the image will be called a duotone, and the printer will set it up for you.

Remove the color. In this process, your image will stay in RGB mode; however, you still need to remove the color. To do this, choose Enhance > Adjust Color > Remove Color.

2 **Add back one color.** In this next step, you will be working with an adjustment layer. Adjustment layers provide a marvelous way to apply edits to your image that are nondestructive—which means that you can go back and change the edits at any time. Click the Layers tab in the palette well to bring up the Layers palette. Click the Adjustment Layers icon located at the bottom of the palette. Choose Hue/Saturation.

Adjust the hue. First, make sure the Colorize box is checked. Then drag the Hue slider until you see your desired color. Experiment with the saturation of the color by dragging the Saturation slider. When you are satisfied with the result, click OK. If you want to change the settings later, double-click the layer thumbnail on the Layers palette.

4 **Save an export version.** Again, save the original; then choose File > Save As, rename the file, and save the file in TIFF format.

3
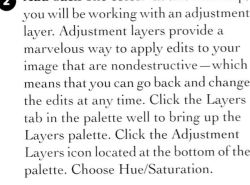

Grayscale

Red Hue

Cyan Hue

Yellow Hue

When using a page layout program such as PageMaker, you can choose an accent color for text, graphics, and images. If you go to a print shop, this will be called a spot color. This process is most commonly referred to as printing a duotone. In choosing your spot color, you should select a color that will work in a variety of tint percentages or shades. Here are some good tips for working with color.

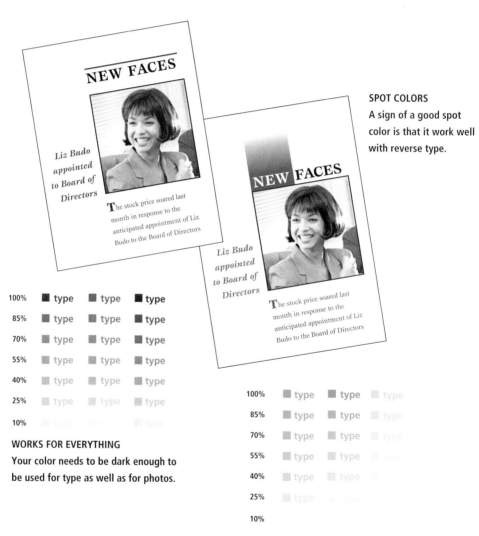

SPOT COLORS
A sign of a good spot color is that it work well with reverse type.

100% type type type
85% type type type
70% type type type
55% type type type
40% type type type
25% type type type
10%

WORKS FOR EVERYTHING
Your color needs to be dark enough to be used for type as well as for photos.

100% type type type
85% type type type
70% type type type
55% type type type
40% type type type
25% type
10%

BEWARE
Light colors such as yellow, orange, and cyan can disappear at tints of less than 80 percent.

Project 8

Create Postcards and Posters

Create great postcards and posters using your own photographs or just Photoshop Elements for your artwork.

This project can be used in a variety of ways. Let's say you want to create a simple postcard for a friend's party. Easy enough: you can either create one from one of the templates provided or create one by combining an image of your choice with one of the templates.

Now let's say you own a nightclub downtown. You want to create a hip postcard that lists upcoming engagements, and you want to create an eye-catching poster along with it. You can do that, too.

Get ready. First, decide if you are going to use a template that calls for your own photograph or one of the template textures. If you are going to use your own photograph, make sure the resolution and size of the image match the resolution and size of the template being used. If you are creating more than one piece, such as a postcard and a poster, you can use the larger image for both pieces.

Open the template you are going to use from the Proj08 folder. Choose File > Save As and save the file with a new name. If you want a double-sided postcard, you will need to open both post_#a and post_#b to create the front and back sides.

Use the postcard gallery to help you decide which template to use. Each postcard has accompanying templates for a flyer and a poster.

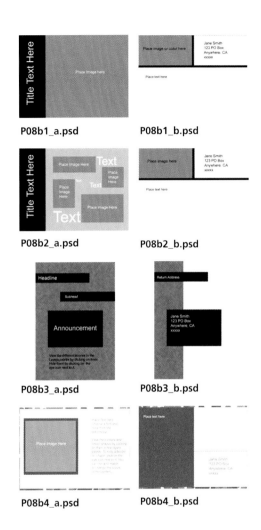

P08b1_a.psd   P08b1_b.psd

P08b2_a.psd   P08b2_b.psd

P08b3_a.psd   P08b3_b.psd

P08b4_a.psd   P08b4_b.psd

②

Edit the template. This example uses the postcard template P08b2_a.psd. To edit the type, bring up the Layers palette by clicking the Layers tab in the palette well.

Double-click the title text layer to select the type. Enter your own text.

③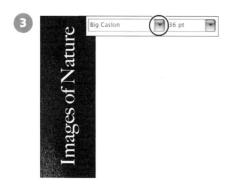

Change the typeface. You will probably want to change the font of the title to match the style of your photo. To change the font, select the text and then choose a new font from the options bar pull-down menu. You can adjust the size at the same time.

④

Color your type. With the type still selected, click the Color swatch on the options bar and choose a color from the color picker. If you want, you can use the Eyedropper tool to pick up a color from your image. The pointer will change to the Eyedropper tool(✐) when it's outside the color picker.

Repeat steps 2, 3, and 4 for any other type layers that may be in the template you are using.

⑤

Shape changes. Depending on the template you are using, there may be some shape layers that you want to alter. For instance, you may want to change the color of the shape layer under the text, as in this example. To change the color of a shape layer, simply double-click the shape layer on the Layers palette. This brings up the Color dialog box. From here, you can either choose a color from the color picker or use the Eyedropper tool to pick up a color from the image.

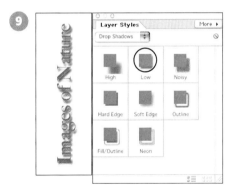

Place your photo. Select the placeholder image layer on the postcard template so that when you place your image, it will be in the proper layer order. Open the image you are going to use in Photoshop Elements. If you have not done so already, check the resolution and size of your image to make sure they match the template. For more information on cropping and image resizing, see "Use the correct image size" on page 3.

Position the template window next to your image window or in a way that you can view both windows. Click the image window to make it active. Select the Move tool (▶⊕) and place the cursor inside the image. Click the image and drag it into the postcard file.

Alternately, select your image and choose Select > All or Ctrl/Cmd+A from the menu bar and then Edit > Copy. Select the postcard file and choose Edit > Paste or Ctrl/Cmd+V.

7 Scale your photo. If your photo is too large, choose Image > Transform > Free Transform. Hold down the Shift key and drag inward on a corner box. Holding down Shift ensures that your photo will stay in proportion.

8 Delete placeholders. When you are finished adding images, delete any remaining placeholder layers. Select the layer and turn off the eye icon, or click the trash icon on the Layers palette.

9

Add some final style. The Style palette in Photoshop Elements allows you to add drop shadows, bevels, textures, and patterns to your layer.

To apply a style to your text, click the text layer, and then click the Layers Styles tab in the palette well.

Note: If you want to keep a palette open, simply drag the palette away from the docking area.

On the Layer Styles palette, click the pop-up menu and select one of the options. Experiment with combining some of the style options, such as a drop shadow with a pattern. To clear a style, click the Clear Style icon () in the upper left corner of the palette. To adjust any of the effects on your layer, choose Layer > Layer Style from the menu bar.

Copy title effects to your photos.
You may want to apply the same effects that you applied to your text to your images. This is a painless operation. Select the text layer; then choose Layer > Layer Effects > Copy Layer Style. Next, select the image layer and choose Layer > Layer Effects > Paste Layer Style. That's it—you're done.

Save and print your card or poster.
Remember: You always want to save a working version of your file. Choose File > Save As and save the file with a new name. To print your file, choose File > Save As and select the Save a

Copy box. Choose TIFF as your file format and save the file with a new name. You are almost ready to print.

To make life a little easier, Photoshop Elements has a feature that will print crop marks. This saves you the time of adding them afterward so that you can trim your printout. To set this up, choose File > Print Preview and click the Show More Options box. Select the Crop Marks box next to Border. You can also specify a border size by clicking Border. You are now ready to print.

If you are printing multiple postcards and would like to save some paper, see Project 3, which describes how to create multiple layouts.

If you have created a double-sided postcard, you should have two files. Unless you are going to use a professional printer, you will need to feed your card stock back through your printer to print the back side.

For tips on card stocks to use, see "Choose paper for postcards" on page 56.

Variation: Create textures

With a little experimentation, you can create your own textures in Photoshop Elements either from scratch or by using a photo. They can be used to complement your images or replace the textures in the templates.

1 **Set the stage.** Open Photoshop Elements and create a new file the size of the template you will be using. If you are using an image, place the image in the new file and move to step 3. If you are working from scratch, go to step 2.

2

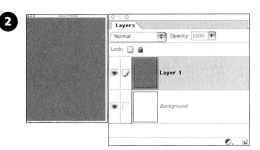

Pick a color. First create a new layer. Click the Layers tab in the docking area to bring up the Layers palette. Click the New Layer icon (▣) and select the new layer that is created. Click the Default Colors icon (▪) and pick a new color using the color picker. Choose Edit > Fill. Under Contents, select Use Foreground Color. Click OK.

3

Add some noise! Select your new layer or image. Click the Filters tab to bring the Filters palette to the front. Note: For this technique, you may want to drag the Filters palette off the palette well so it will stay open.

If you are starting with an image, this step is optional, but if you are starting from scratch, it's a must. Double-click the Add Noise filter and make sure that the Preview box is checked.

Experiment with the settings. This example uses the default Amount setting and the Gaussian distribution. The Monochromatic setting is turned off to get more colors in the mix. Make your own choices; then click OK when you are satisfied.

4

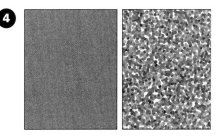

Use those filters. It's not always easy to use the filters in everyday image correction. When you are creating textures, however, they are absolutely essential.

Grant yourself full license to go crazy and experiment with various combinations of filters to see what you like and what works best. The example here uses Colored Pencil and Pointalize. When you are finished creating your new texture, choose File > Save As and save your file with a new name in a TIFF format. It is now ready to be placed in the template of your choice.

Before printing your postcard, you will want to think about your paper thickness and texture. The minimum thickness you can use for mailing a stand-alone card is 7 points. Most 7-point stock is uncoated, meaning not glossy. You will also need to think about what can go through your printer unless you are using a professional printing house.

The other option for postcards is an 8-point stock coated on one side (commonly referred to as 8-point C1S). The advantage to using a card stock that is glossy on one side is that the image will look good, and you can still write on the other side.

Paper stock that is coated on one side comes in thicknesses of 8, 10, 12, and 14 points. You should run a test sheet through your printer if you are printing at home. You can find heavier stock, but it is often too heavy to use in many printers (even professional ones).

Tools:

Photoshop Elements

Materials:

Your image and fabric

Templates

Phototransfer paper

Project 9

Create T-Shirts, Tote Bags, and More!

Use the project templates and phototransfer paper to place images on T-shirts, tote bags, and other fabrics.

Have you wanted to create your own T-shirt design, maybe for a sports team or special event? This project gives you the templates for adding images, logos, and slogans to T-shirts and other items. All you need are your images, ideas, and phototransfer paper.

1 Check the size of your artwork. Depending on what you're creating, you may have a few different types of files. For example, if you are creating something for a sports team, you may have logo artwork, or you may be using your new baby's photograph on a tote bag for grandma.

In either case, the logo or image dimensions need to be approximately 6 x 9 inches with a resolution of 150 pixels per inch. The exact dimensions will vary depending on the template you use, so look at the template size first. To check the resolution and size of your image in Photoshop Elements, choose Image > Resize > Image Size. For more information see "Use the correct image size" on page 3.

Artwork that is vector based, such as an Adobe Illustrator file, can be resized inside the template.

Edit your photograph. Open the photograph that you want to use in Photoshop Elements. Make any color corrections and other edits that the photo may need.

3 Save two versions. After you have finished making edits to your image, choose File > Save As. Rename the file and save it in a Photoshop format. This will save any layers in the file in case you want to make changes later.

Next, choose File > Save As and select TIFF as the format. Save the file with the .tif suffix so you don't replace the working version. Close the file.

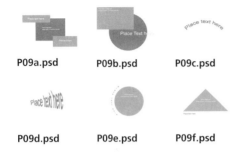

P09a.psd   P09b.psd   P09c.psd

P09d.psd   P09e.psd   P09f.psd

(4)

Edit the template. In the Project 9 folder, open the template that you want to use in Photoshop Elements and save it with a new name. If the Layers palette is not visible, click the Layers tab in the palette well. Notice that there is a text layer for a slogan or company saying on the Layers palette.

Double-click the text layer to select the text. Enter your own message or company slogan. Change the font and size using the pop-up menus on the Type options bar. To change the color of the text, click the color swatch on the Type options bar. Select a new color using the color picker that appears; then click OK. For information on editing template colors and image masks see Projects 8 and 11.

(5)

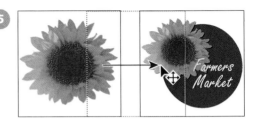

Place and size your artwork. Use one of the following techniques to place your artwork.

• For photographs: Open the TIFF file you saved earlier in Photoshop Elements and place the window next to the template window. Using the Move tool (▶⊕), drag the photograph into the template.

• For vector artwork such as logos: Choose File > Place. Navigate to your file and click Place. Use the handles to resize the image after it is placed in the template. After you place the artwork, use the Move tool to position it.

(6) **Save and print your file.** Repeat step 3 and save two versions of the new file: one Photoshop version and one TIFF version for printing. After saving the file, choose File > Print to print your file on phototransfer paper. Note: Different manufacturers of phototransfer papers have different printing setup requirements. Follow the manufacturer's instructions.

Printing a mirror image

Read the detailed instructions that come with the phototransfer paper. Most papers work from a mirror image so that the image and text will be correct when ironed onto a fabric. If your printer does not have a mirror or reverse setting, use the following steps to create a mirror image.

1 In your TIFF file, choose Image > Rotate > Flip Horizontal.

2 Choose File > Print and print according to the instructions of the paper manufacturer.

Prepping the fabric

- ○ Prewash the material to remove any residual chemicals.

- ○ Rinse clean with no softeners or additives.

Ironing

- ○ Preheat the Iron using the highest setting and drain any water from steam irons.

- ○ A normal ironing board is too soft so use a low, hard surface such as a counter or table at waist or knee level. This allows you to lean over the iron and exert strong pressure along with the high heat. DO NOT USE A GLASS TABLE!

- ○ Place a wrinkle-free pillowcase on the ironing surface. Center the transfer area of your fabric over the pillowcase.

Tools:

Photoshop Elements

Materials:

*Cover templates for CDs,
binders, and videos*

Your photos

Project 10

Blend Multiple Images to Create Covers for CDs, Binders, and Videos

*Give your covers a striking look by blending imagery,
text, and graphics.*

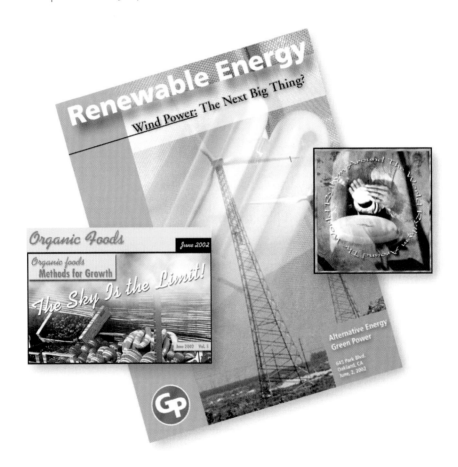

Have you ever seen a collage of images that, pieced together, meant more than each image separately? Such a grouping is often used to tell a story or to make a visual connection for the viewer.

In this project, you will blend two separate images together to create one illustration. You will then combine this image with text and graphics to create a cover for a CD, binder, or video.

Get started. Open the Photoshop Elements template that you want to use for the project. There are three types of templates: for a CD cover, a binder cover, and a video cover. They are located in the Project 10 folder. After you have opened your template, open the images you plan to blend together.

Size your images. Look at the template file to determine the exact resolution and dimensions for your images. The resolution needs to be the same for both images. For tips on image resizing and resolution, see "Use the correct image size" on page 3.

Copy and paste. Click the image you want in the foreground of your illustration and choose Select > All (Ctrl/Cmd+A) to select everything; then choose Edit > Copy (Ctrl/Cmd+C). At this point, you can close the file.

Select the background image and choose Edit > Paste (Ctrl/Cmd+V). You now have two separate layers in your file, each containing one image. To see your Layers palette, click the Layers tab in the palette well. To make it stay open, drag it off the palette well. You may want to keep this palette open so you can always see what is happening.

Save a backup version. As always, you should have a working file that contains all of your layers. Choose File > Save As and save your work in a new file with a different name in Photoshop format. This ensures that you can always go back to your original work and make new edits.

Create a new layer with a mask.
You will now create a new top layer with a layer mask. The layer mask will be the agent for blending the two layers. Follow these steps:

• Select the top layer.

• Choose Edit > Select All (Ctrl/Cmd+A).

• Choose Edit > Copy (Ctrl/Cmd+V).

• Choose Edit > Paste Into (Ctrl/Cmd+Shift+V).

• Choose Layer > New > Layer via Copy (Ctrl/Cmd+J).

Your new layer should have an empty box to the right of it on the Layers palette. This is the layer mask. Hide the original top layer by clicking the eye icon.

Create the blend of two images.
You next need to paint in the layer mask so the bottom layer can show through. This can be done in a variety of ways, but here you will use the Gradient tool. For other methods, see the variations at the end of the project.

First, click the layer mask on the Layers palette. A little mask icon ( ) appears next to the eye icon on the palette. This lets you know that you are working in the mask and not in the image.

Choose the Gradient tool (▭) from the toolbox. On the options bar, click the gradient picker to choose a gradient. Select the default black-and-white or black-to-transparent gradient. A mask can be only in grayscale. Whereever black is applied in the image mask, the image will be hidden, and the opposite is true for white. By using a gradient, you are creating a soft blend of the two images.

The default gradient type is Linear. This is a good type to start with. Place the cursor on one side the image and then drag to the other side.

Adjusting the amount or angle of the blend is easy. Just make sure that your mask is selected and then drag with the Gradient tool from different areas of the image until you are satisfied with the results. Experiment with other types of gradients such as Radial, Reflected, and Diamond.

Choose File > Save.

Place the image in the template.
Make sure that your top layer is selected. Choose Select > All (Ctrl/Cmd+A) and then Edit > Copy Merged. Click the template that you opened at the beginning of the project to make it active. Select the bottom layer and choose Edit > Paste (Ctrl/Cmd+V).

Add your text. Double-click the Title layer; the text should be selected. Enter your own title. Repeat this process for any other text layers in the template. If there is text that you don't want, click the eye icon next to it to hide it. To

move the title or any other text, select the Move tool (⯈⊕) and drag the text to the position you want.

 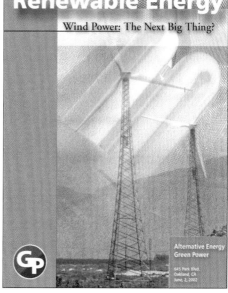

Adjust colors and styles. You will probably want to change the color of the shapes or text to match your image better. To change the color of the text, select the Text tool (T) and click the text layer. Then click the color swatch on the options bar, and use the color picker to choose a new color for your text.

Changing the color of a shape is just as easy. Just double-click the shape layer and use the color picker to choose your color.

10 **Save working and export versions of the image.** Save your working file. Then choose File > Save a Copy, rename the file, and save it in TIFF format.

Variation: Select creatively

A. No mask **B. Using the Leaf Brush**

Make creative selections. You don't have to use the regular Marquee tool to make your selection. Try using the selection brush and experiment with different brushes. Remember that when you are using the Paintbrush tool, black adds to the mask, and white takes away from the mask.

Variation: Change Modes

A. No mask **B. Screen mode**

Try a new mode. It can also be fun to experiment with different Layer modes.

Blending images can be a tricky process. Often, it's good to work with one image that creates more of a pattern and one that is the focal point. How you treat your text and titles can greatly affect the final image as well.

OPPOSITES DO ATTRACT!
When blending images, it often works well to have one of the images be more of a texture or more abstract than the other.

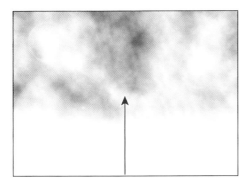

A GRADUAL PROCESS
In this example, a linear gradient works well to create a gradual blend with the image below.

THE RIGHT TYPE
This friendly script works well with the subject matter of organic food.

Tools:

Photoshop Elements
PageMaker (optional)

Materials:

Mask templates
Ad template
Your photo

Project 11

Create a Black-and-White Ad for Publication

Create a professional advertisement for use in a black-and-white publication.

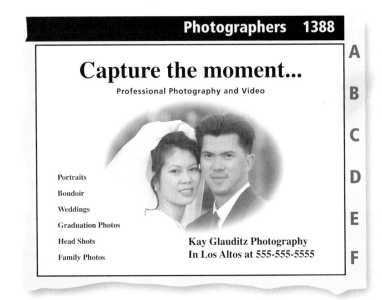

You can use Photoshop Elements to create your own advertisements. In this project, you will use a template to create a typical advertisement that can be used in a black-and-white publication. All you need is your own photo; the template provides the mask and text block. Note: The CD contains an optional PageMaker template that can be used for placing text.

Get started. Open your image in Photoshop Elements.

Trim and resize the photo. For the purposes of this template, the photograph needs to be 130 points high and 175 points wide, with a resolution of 144 pixels per inch (for more information see "Use the correct image size" on page 3).

Make the photo black and white. Choose Image > Mode > Grayscale and then click OK.

You may notice a loss of contrast and tonal range going from color to grayscale. If this is the case, choose Enhance > Adjust Brightness/Contrast > Levels. Drag the triangular sliders under Input Levels to adjust the tonal range. Make sure the Preview box is checked so you can see what is happening to your image.

(For more information on levels, refer to the Photoshop Elements User Guide.)

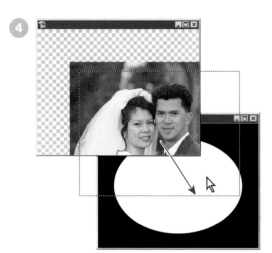

Place your photo in the template.
Open one of a templates in the Proj11
folder. (Use P11a.psd for an oval
photo, and P11b.psd for a rectangular
photo.) The illustration here shows the
drag-and-drop technique. To use this
technique, arrange the image and
template windows so that you can see
both of them at the same time.

Select the Move tool (⬆) and Shift-
drag your photo into the mask template. Release the mouse when the
template window becomes highlighted.
This technique places a centered copy
of your image in the template. You can
also copy and paste your image into the
template.

Select the mask. If it is not already
visible, bring up the Layers palette by
clicking the Layers tab in the palette
well. You may want to drag the Layers
palette off the palette well to keep it
open. On the Layers palette, Ctrl/
Cmd+click the Oval or Rectangle layer
to select the mask shape.

Subtract the mask shape from your image. You are going to delete the mask shape from your image, but first you need to feather the edge of your selection. Select your photo layer on the Layers palette and then choose Select > Feather, enter 8 to create a nice soft edge, and click OK.

Press Delete or Backspace to delete the selection from the photo. Hide the Oval or Rectangle layer by clicking the eye icon on the Layers palette. As you can see, feathering the selection gives a softer edge to the selection outline.

Save two versions of your file. Remember to always save a working version of your file that contains all of your layers. To do this, choose File > Save As, rename the file, and save it in Photoshop format. Next, save a flattened (no layers) version for export. Choose File > Save As, check the Save a Copy box, and save the file in TIFF format with a new name.

You can now use the TIFF version in either the Elements ad template or the PageMaker ad template. The following steps assume that you are using the template in Photoshop Elements.

Choose your template. There are three ad layout templates in Photoshop Elements: P11c, d, and e. Open the one you want to use along with the TIFF file you just saved.

Place your new photograph. Arrange the two files so that you see both of them. Using the drag-and-drop technique that you used earlier, place the TIFF file in the template.

Replace the text with your own. Double-click the text layers to select the text and enter your own copy. You can change the fonts on the text options bar to match the style of your ad.

Again, save a working version with all of the layers in case you want to make any changes later. After you have a working version saved, save your file in TIFF format using a different name.

Have you ever noticed how some advertisements really jump off the page: Did you immediately know whom the target customer was? Was it visually striking and compelling? These are some questions you want your own audience to answer yes to when you are creating an advertisement for any type of promotional purpose. The following tips offer some good advice for creating effective ads.

KEEP IT BRIEF
A short, strong headline captures the attention of your customers and makes them interested in what you have to say.

LESS IS MORE
Try to avoid a cluttered image. White space gives the message more impact.

MAKE A CHANGE
Use a different font to highlight critical points, such as your business name or phone number.

USE STRONG IMAGERY
It's best not to use a photo that has too much going on.

Project 12

Create Photographic Backgrounds for Slide Presentations

Make your next presentation more exciting by using Photoshop Elements to create photographic backdrops.

This project is for you presentation artists who want to expand beyond the usual templates and bullet points that come with slide presentations. Photographic backgrounds can put your presentation text into a context — something your audience, whether they know it or not, will appreciate. With this technique, you can create your backdrop in Photoshop Elements and then finish the slide in a presentation application, or you can create a PDF slideshow right in Photoshop Elements in a technique discussed later in this book (see Project 14).

1 Get started. Open the photograph you want to use for a slide background in Photoshop Elements.

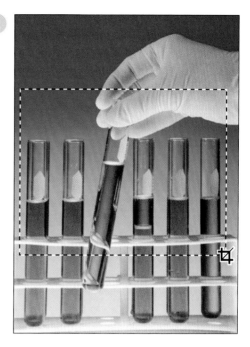

Trim and size the photo. Use the Crop tool to resize the photo to a height of 480 pixels and a width of 640 pixels. The resolution should be 72 pixels per inch (see "Use the correct image size" on page 3). These dimensions will allow you to produce a full-screen display for monitors and online projectors. If you work with an outside vendor to create or output your slides, check to find out the size the vendor uses.

3 Create a new shape. If it's not already visible, bring up the Layers palette by clicking the Layers tab in the palette well. Select the Rectangle tool from the toolbox and drag inside the image. Don't worry about the color just yet.

This rectangle is going to become a semitransparent shape over the image area in which to place your text.

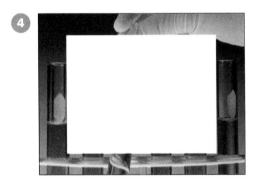

Change the shape color. To change the color of your shape layer, double-click the shape on the Layers palette. Choose white from the color picker.

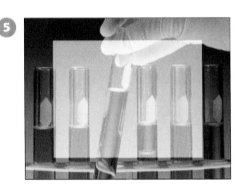

Screen back the layer. Make sure that your shape layer is selected on the Layers palette. Using the opacity slider, change the opacity setting to 50 percent.

6 Save two versions. As always, save a working version of your file that contains all of your new layers. This will allow you to easily go back and make adjustments and changes if you need to. To use the file in another program, you will want a single-layer version. Choose File > Save As and select the Save a Copy check box. Under Format, choose TIFF or a format supported by your presentation application; then save the file with a new name.

Variation: Use different shapes

Leave the box behind. You can place your text inside ovals or hand-drawn shapes. Experiment with some of the other shape tools. To access the other shape tools, hold down the mouse on the Rectangle tool.

Variation: Transform the container

Here are some quick shortcuts to transform, rotate, or distort a shape.

• To scale and center the shape layer, hold down Alt/Option and drag a handle.

• To rotate the shape, place the pointer outside the bounding box and drag in the direction you want to rotate.

• To distort freely, press Ctrl/Cmd and drag a handle.

• To skew, press Ctrl/Cmd+Shift and drag a side handle.

- To apply perspective, press Ctrl+Alt+Shift/Cmd+Option+Shift and drag a corner handle.

- To undo the last change, choose Edit > Undo.

Press Enter to apply the transformation or Esc to cancel the transformation.

Variation: Use an image color for your shape layer

Pick up a color from your image and use it for your shape layer. Double-click your shape layer to bring up the color picker. Move the cursor into the image area to get the Eyedropper tool (🖋). Click to sample a color in the image; then click OK.

Variation: Soften the edges

If the look you are after is a more gradual edge, then use this technique. One word of caution: your shape layer will need to be changed from vector based to pixel based, so make this your final step.

Select your shape layer and choose Filter > Blur > Gaussian Blur. A dialog box will appear telling you that the layer needs to be simplified for this filter. Click OK and proceed to the next dialog box to create your Gaussian Blur.

When you use a photographic background, try to find an interesting image that relates to the topic of your presentation. Choose neutral colors to act as your text boxes to ensure good readability. White can be very effective because it acts as a subtle tint of the original colors in the image.

DON'T
Watch where you place your shapes. Avoid awkward areas such as over a person's face.

DON'T
If you place your shape too low on a slide, it will be lopsided or cut off when it's projected.

DO
Try to center the shape in your image area.
Choose View > Rulers for precise measurement guides.

Project 13

Create Photographic Sidebars
for Professional-Looking Slides

Use photographs to create sidebars or backdrops to make your online presentations more dynamic.

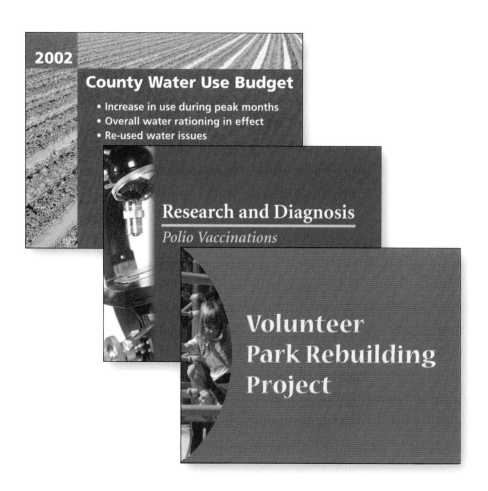

Photographic sidebars can give your presentation a visual frame that places the main text, graphs, or charts within a context. The center of the slide remains available for informational content, with the photograph seen only on the edges. Using provided sidebar templates, you can create numerous photographic effects for online slides.

① **Get started.** Open your photo file in Photoshop Elements; then open the sidebar template you want to use. The Proj13 folder contains eight templates, each with a different sidebar shape and layout.

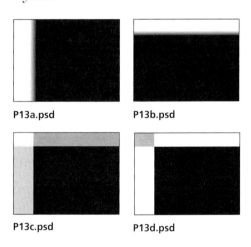

P13a.psd   P13b.psd

P13c.psd   P13d.psd

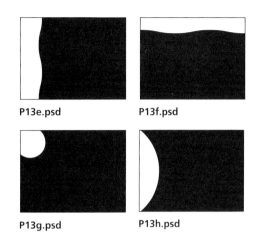

P13e.psd   P13f.psd

P13g.psd   P13h.psd

② **Size the photo.** To use these templates, you will need to crop and resize the photo to at least 480 pixels high or 640 pixels wide. You may need to do both depending on the template you choose. The photo resolution needs to be 72 pixels per inch (see "Use the correct image size" on page 3).

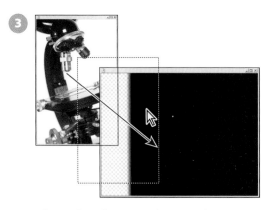

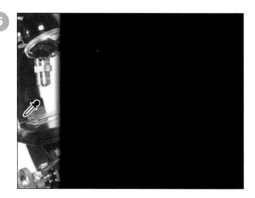

Place the photo in the template.
Arrange the photo and template windows side by side, or so that you can see both of them. Click the photo window to make it active and then select the Move tool (▶⊕). Use the Move tool to drag the photo into the sidebar template. When a highlight appears around the template window, release the mouse button. This will drop a copy of the photo into the template window. You can reposition the photo in the template by dragging it with the Move tool.

Select a color for the body of the slide. Select the Eyedropper tool (✐) from the toolbox and click in the photo to sample a color for the body of the slide. The sampled color will appear in the Foreground color swatch (■).

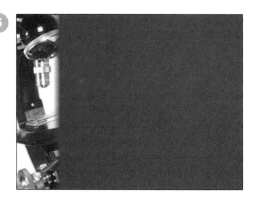

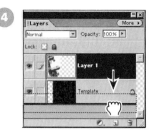

Arrange the layers. If your Layers palette is not showing, click the Layers tab in the palette well. On the Layers palette, drag the photo layer to the bottom of the list.

Color the slide body. Select the Template layer on the Layers palette, and choose Edit > Fill. When the dialog box appears, choose Foreground Color for the contents; then click OK.

7 **Save two versions of the file.** It's always a good idea to save a working version of your file in case you want to make changes. To save a working version with all of the layers, choose File > Save As, rename the file, and save the file in Photoshop format. To save a single-layer version for export, choose File > Save As and select the Save a Copy check box. Rename the file and save it in TIFF format or in a format supported by your presentation application.

Variation: Change the position of the sidebar template

To create a number of different looks, try changing the orientation of a template. For example, by flipping the template, you can make the sidebar appear along the left or the right or along the top or the bottom of the slide. To change the orientation of a template, choose Image > Rotate > Flip Vertical or Flip Horizontal.

Original template   **Flip Horizontal**

Variation: Add texture to the sidebar template

Use the texture filter to add a texture to your sidebar templates.

Apply a texture. After coloring the slide body in step 6 of the project, click the Filters tab in the palette well. Click the pop-up menu and choose Texture. Now you will see only the filters that apply textures. If you are in List view, click the More pop-up menu and select Thumbnail View to see a preview of all of the textures.

Make sure that the Template layer is selected on the Layers palette and click a texture filter. To apply the filter, either click Apply or double-click the filter. If you want to try another filter, choose Edit > Undo (Ctrl/Cmd+Z).

DESIGN TIP: Choose colors for the slide body

Selecting the right color for the body of your slide can be critical. Start by looking at your presentation needs. Every different body color produces a different reading effect and overall feel.

STAY NEUTAL
Neutral, subdued colors promote the visibility of the slide contents and work well with the provided texture actions.

TOO BRIGHT
Bright, vivid colors may make text difficult to read.

Tools:

Photoshop Elements

Materials:

Your photos

Project 14

Create a PDF Slideshow

Create an automated computer slideshow using the
PDF Slideshow feature of Photoshop Elements.

The PDF Slideshow feature is terrific for creating a personal or professional slideshow for an online or desktop presentation.

① **Organize your images.** First make the necessary edits to the images you plan to use in the slideshow.

The slideshow will be shown full screen, so for the best image quality the size should be at least 1280 x 1024 with a resolution of 72 pixels per inch. (For more information on sizing your images see "Use the correct image size" on page 3). After you are through editing the images, place them all in one folder for easy access.

②

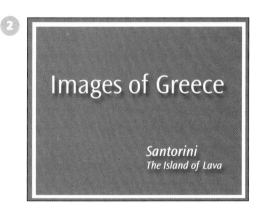

Create your title slide. In Photoshop Elements, choose File > New. For Height and Width, enter the same pixel values that you used for your slide images. The resolution should still be 72.

In the new file, select the color that you want to use for the background by clicking the Default Color icon (■). Select a color from the color picker that appears. Then click the Paint Bucket tool (⬧) and click anywhere in the image.

Finally, select the Type tool (T). Position the cursor in the center of the image. Click to enter your title text.

③ **Change the font and text color.** Double-click to select the text. On the options bar, use the pop-up menus to select different fonts and sizes. To change the color, simply click the color swatch on the options bar and use the color picker to select a new color.

Choose File > Save As and save the file in the Photoshop format in case you want to make changes later. Be sure to save it in the same folder as your other images. Note: To find out about creating a title slide with a photographic background, see Project 12.

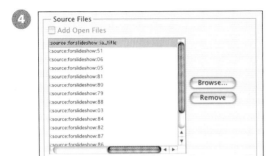

Choose the slideshow images.
Choose File > Automation Tools > PDF Slideshow. Under Source Files, click Browse and navigate to the folder that contains your images. Select the folder and click Open.

When you are inside the folder, hold down the Shift key to select multiple images. After you have selected all of the images, click Open.

In the PDF Slideshow Source window, you will see a list of images. The slideshow will start with the image at the top of the list. You can reorder the images by clicking and dragging them into the correct sequence.

Save your slideshow. Under Output File, click Choose. At this point, you can save your file as Slideshow.pdf or save it with a new name.

Set up your final options. In the Slide Show Options area, you are going to set up your advance timing, looping, and transitions.

The default setting for advancing the images is 5 seconds. If your slides are images only, this may be too long. If your slides have any text, this may be too short. Decide what time works best for your slides and enter that value. If you want the slideshow to repeat after it's finished, then select the Loop after Last Page check box.

Finally, choose the transition that you want to occur between slides. You may want to experiment to see which you like best.

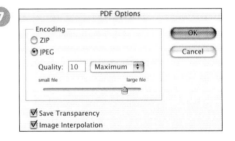

Choose your compression. Click Advanced. This brings you to the PDF compression settings. The default setting is JPEG with a quality of Maximum. If you are posting this slideshow to the Web, you might want to make the Quality setting lower, to create a smaller file. The rest of the default settings are fine. Click OK to create your slideshow — and you're done.

Project 15

Create a Web Photo Gallery

Using nothing but your photographs and Photoshop Elements, you can create a sophisticated online gallery.

If you want to quickly post a gallery of images online, the Web Photo Gallery is just the thing. Photoshop Elements will create all of the HTML files as well as size and compress your images for the Web. The only thing you need to do is put you gallery on your server.

Note: Photoshop Elements gives your HTML files the suffix .html or .htm. If you are uncertain which to use, choose .htm.

1 Organize your image files. First make the necessary edits to the images you will be posting to the Web.

Photoshop Elements will resize the images and compress a copy of them for the Web. To be sure you don't accidently compress them twice, save the edited files in a PSD format. (For more information on compression formats, go to the online help in Photoshop Elements.)

After you are finished editing the images, place them in one folder for easy access. This will become your source folder.

Next, create a new folder. Give it a name that designates it as the destination for the final image and HTML files.

Select a gallery style. In Photoshop Elements, choose File > Create Web Photo Gallery. You first task is to set the style of the gallery.

Click the pop-up Styles menu. When you select a style, a preview of it appears on the right side of the Web Gallery dialog box.

Some of the styles already have a finished look, while others are simple and allow for customizing. Select one that will work well with your images.

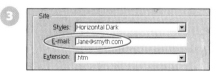

Enter your e-mail address (optional). In the E-mail text box, enter your e-mail address. The address will be a link in the title banner of the gallery.

4 Set your source and destination. Under Folders, click Browse/Choose. Navigate to the folder containing all of your images. Select the folder and click OK/Choose. Do the same for Destination, only this time choose the destination folder you created in step 1.

⑤

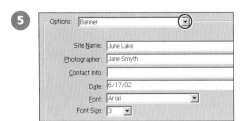

Create your title banner. Click the pop-up Options menu and select Banner. Enter the gallery title, the photographer's name, and the contact information.

⑥

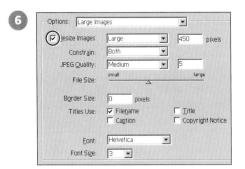

Set up your images. Click the Options pop-up menu again and choose Large Images. This dialog box is where you enter the size and compression you want to use when saving your Web images. Follow these steps for both the large images and image thumbnails:

• Make sure that the Resize Images check box is checked. On the pop-up menu next to it, you can choose Large (450 pixels), Medium (350 pixels), Small (250 pixels), or Custom. Select the size that you want. From the Constrain pop-up menu, specify

whether you want your image size to be constrained horizontally or vertically.

• For JPEG Quality, select the setting that will work best with your images. Keep in mind that when you're saving JPEG images for the Web, medium or even low quality can be adequate. Higher-quality images that look great mean larger file sizes, and files that take longer to load on the screen.

• For Border Size, enter the pixel value you want for a border. If you don't want a border, enter 0.

• Select the check boxes for the text you want used as the image title. Titles, captions, and any copyright information will be taken from File Info, located on the File menu. Select the font and font size for the text.

⑦ **Set up security (optional).** The Security option is the last menu item on the Options pop-up menu.

The Security settings allow you to enter custom text, text for copyright information, titles, captions, and credits. To enter this information, select Security from the Options pop-up menu; then select an option from the Content pop-menu.

Variation: Change your colors

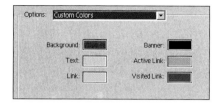

Customize the colors. If you used one of the basic frame or table styles for your gallery, you can easily customize the colors.

From the Options pop-up menu, select Custom Colors. Click the color swatches to change the colors of the text, links, background, and gallery banner.

Variation: Use an image for your background

Use your own background. This technique can be used only with the Table style. To use an image for the background, you need to have an image saved in JPEG format. Select Background under Folders and navigate to the image you want to use for the background. For more information on using background images, see Project 17.

Project 16

Create a Web Banner

Use your logo and message to create simple yet effective banners for your Web site.

Creating a banner using your company logo is a good way to get the attention of customers and establish an identity on the Web. In this project, you create a great-looking banner using an existing template.

Get started. Open one of the banner templates in the Proj16 folder in Photoshop Elements. The background area is 468 pixels by 60 pixels—this is the most common Web banner size.

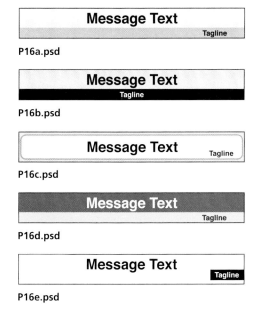

P16a.psd

P16b.psd

P16c.psd

P16d.psd

P16e.psd

Place your logo. Choose File > Place and navigate to your company logo. Select the file and click Place.

You can use the Place feature for EPS files, Adobe Illustrator files, and Adobe Acrobat PDF files. If you have more images that you want to place that are not in one of these formats, use the copy technique described in Project 6 (see "Place your image within the border." on page 38).

If your Layers palette is not showing, click the Layers tab in the palette well. The Layers palette now has at least four layers: one for your logo, one called Message Text, one called Tagline, and a background layer. (Some templates have layers for more than one background color.) If you have imported other artwork, layers for that artwork will also appear.

Replace the text. Double-click the Message Text layer to select it. After the text is selected, enter your own text to replace it. Use the options bar to edit the font, size, and color. Repeat this step to edit the text on the Tagline layer.

Move the logo and artwork into position. Select the logo's layer and use the Move tool (⬏) to position the logo. Repeat this step to arrange any other pieces of artwork in the banner.

5 **Customize the colors.** You may want to alter the colors of the background to match your logo and other artwork.

To do this, select the background layer you want to change. Then click the foreground color swatch in the toolbox and use the color picker to select a color you like. Using the Paint Bucket tool (), click the area of color you want to change. Repeat this step for any other background colors you want to change.

6 **Save working and Web-optimized versions.** Choose File > Save As and save a working version of the file with a new name. Make sure it is in PSD format; this way, all of the layers will be there in case you want to make changes later.

Variation: Make your logo move!

This technique allows you to animate your logo by using the Layers palette. Because each layer becomes an individual frame in the animation, it is easier to start by animating just one object such as a logo. The example shows how to move the logo across the banner, but with a little experimentation and practice, you can create all sorts of animation.

Copy the logo layer. Make sure you have saved a working version of your file; then delete all of the layers except the one with your logo.

Select the logo layer and drag it over the Create a New Layer icon (⬛) located at the bottom of the Layers palette. There should now be two logo layers, including one named copy. Repeat this step until you have made four or five copies of your logo layer. These layers will become the frames in your animation.

2

Create the animation frames. Photoshop Elements will display the frames in the stacking order of the layers, meaning that the bottom layer will be your first frame, and so forth. For the purpose of this example, the bottom layer will be referred to as layer 1, and each subsequent layer will be called layer 2, layer 3, and so on. To rename a layer, just double-click the layer and enter a new name in the Layer Properties box.

Select layer 1 and use the Move tool
(➤⊕) to place it at the far right side of
the banner. This will be your first
frame. Next, select layer 2 and move it
to the left of layer 1. Repeat this process
for the remaining layers until the final
frame is in place.

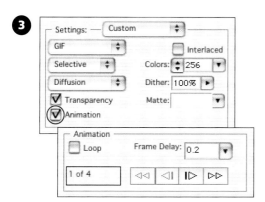

Finish and preview your animation.
Choose File > Save for Web. Make sure
that the format is set to GIF and the
Animation check box is checked.

Set your animation speed using the
Frame Delay pop-up menu located at
the bottom of the Save for Web dialog
box. If you want your animation to
loop, select the Loop check box.

Preview your animation by clicking the
Preview In icon at the bottom of the
dialog box. This gives a preview of the
animation in the default Web browser.

4 **Save your animation.** When you are
satisfied with your animation, click OK
and save it with a new name.

When creating a Web banner, think of it as a highway billboard: simple, big, and eye-catching. Here are a few tips to get you moving in the right direction.

BIG AND BOLD
When choosing your font, try to use simple, clean, sans-serif or bold fonts.

KEEP IT MINIMAL
Watch how much information is being crammed into a tiny space. Less is usually more.

A critical factor when saving images for the Web is file size. Even though many people now have high-speed access to the Web, it's still a good idea to make your pages load fast. A good banner size to aim for is 12 to 15K.

Compare different optimization settings

The Save for Web dialog box has two image windows. One shows you the original image, and one is a preview using the selected optimization settings. Compare different settings until you are satisfied with the quality and size of the optimized version.

Optimize flat-color or animated images

For flat-color images with few colors (such as logos and typefaces) or animated images, use the GIF format.

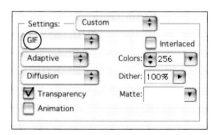

○ Check the status bar at the bottom of the image window to see the file size using the current settings.

○ Try using fewer colors by choosing a value from the Colors pop-up menu on the Optimize palette. Look at the image quality and file size as you try different settings. Often with flat color images, you can use as few as four colors.

Optimize photographs

For photographs and continuous-tone images with color gradations, use the JPEG format.

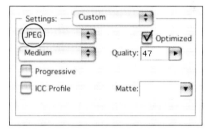

Control the amount of compression by dragging the Quality slider. The higher the quality, the less the compression, and the bigger the file size. Look at the file size as you try different quality levels.

Project 17

Create a Large Background for Your Web Pages

Use a photo or illustration to make a large background for pages on your Web site.

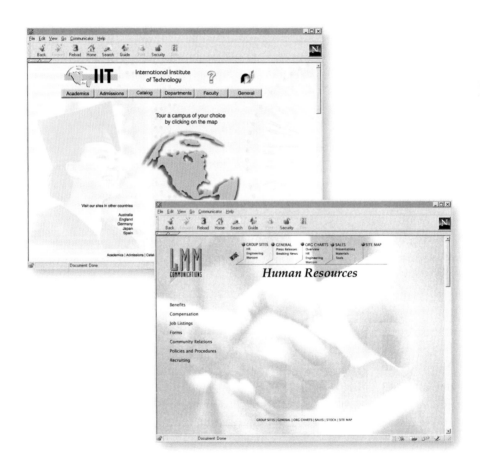

If you have ever wanted to add an interesting background to your Web pages, this technique works great. Using a full-color image to fill the entire background of a Web page would normally result in a file that's too large for Web viewing. In this project, you create a monochromatic background with a small file size that won't slow down your Web pages.

Get started. Open your color photo in Photoshop Elements and resize it as necessary. Generally, for an image to fill the entire background of a Web page, it should be 600 to 800 pixels wide and at least 480 pixels high. The image size you choose should be based on the amount of material on the page. Also remember that background images will tile on the Web unless you set the page to not scroll.

For information on resizing images, see "Use the correct image size" on page 3.

Convert a copy of your background layer to black and white. If your Layers palette is not showing, click the Layers tab in the palette well. Select your background layer and drag it over the Create a New Layer icon(⬜) located at the bottom of the Layers palette. With your new layer selected, choose Enhance > Adjust Color > Remove Color.

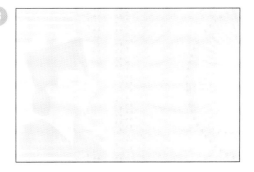

Create a new color layer. You will use this color layer to colorize your black-and-white background. Choose Layer > New Fill Layer > Solid Color. In the New Layer dialog box, select Screen from the Mode pop-up menu and click OK. Then choose a color using the color picker that appears. Remember that this is your primary background color so select a color that will complement the rest of your artwork.

4

Adjust the color opacity. Select the new color layer on the Layers palette. Use the Opacity slider at the top of the palette to adjust the layer's opacity. This affects the intensity of the color and allows more of the grayscale image to show through.

5 **Save a working version of the file.** Choose File > Save As and save the file in Photoshop format using a new name. This way, you will always have a version that contains all of your layers in case you want to make any changes.

6

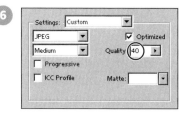

Optimize the image for the Web. After you have saved the working version, choose File > Save for Web. In the Save for Web dialog box, you will see two images. One is the original, and one is a preview of the optimized version. When you select different optimization settings, the changes will be reflected in this preview window.

Select JPEG from the Settings pop-up menu in the upper right corner of the dialog box. Use the Quality slider to adjust the amount the image is compressed. The higher the quality of the image, the larger the file size. Since you are posting this slideshow on the Web, you need to keep the file size small. With this in mind, start with a quality setting of 15. Check the file size underneath the image preview.

Try to keep the file size to around 20K or less. When you are happy with the quality and file size, click OK to save the Web version.

Variation: Experiment with textures!

Use a filter from the Filters palette to add interesting effects and texture to your background. Preview the filters by clicking the Filters tab in the palette well. (If you want to keep the Filters palette open, drag it out of the palette well.)

To apply a filter, select your grayscale background layer; then double-click the filter you want to apply. If the result is not what you want, select Edit > Undo (Ctrl/Cmd+Z).

Adding outside graphic elements to your background image that complement the other graphics on your Web page can make your page more dynamic. Set the page size (and content) so that the background won't tile.

KEEP IT CLEAR
Don't allow the elements in the background to interfere with the page content.

THE FEWER THE BETTER
You need only a couple of colors. Less color helps keep down the file size.

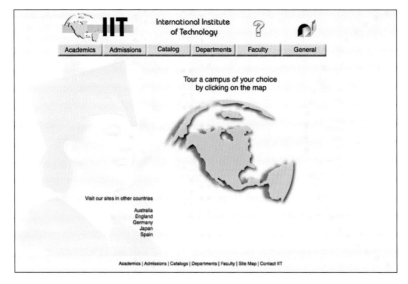

Use graphics that work with or complement the other graphics referenced by your Web page. Exact alignment is not necessary, as the placement of your other elements may vary a few pixels from browser to browser.

A color that is too dark or saturated decreases the legibility of text and can be distracting.

A soft or more neutral background color helps show off the rest of your content.

Project 18

Create Buttons for the Web

Use photos or textures to create buttons for a Web page and buttons that have on and off states.

In this project, you create textured buttons that you can use on a Web page. The texture can be a photograph or one that is already supplied. You will create a textured button, add the text, and save the button as a GIF file. You will also create button rollover states — with different effects for on and off — using layer effects.

1 **Get started.** Open a photo or one of the several texture files in the Proj18 folder in Photoshop Elements. This will be the texture of the button. Resize or crop the image to the desired button size. For information on image resizing, see "Use the correct image size" on page 3.

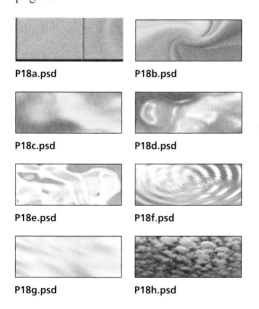

P18a.psd   P18b.psd

P18c.psd   P18d.psd

P18e.psd   P18f.psd

P18g.psd   P18h.psd

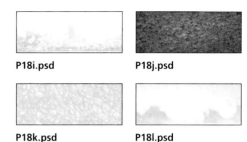

P18i.psd   P18j.psd

P18k.psd   P18l.psd

2

Create a beveled edge. Click the Layers Styles tab and choose Bevels from the pop-up menu. Click one of the bevel styles to apply it to the button. If you don't like the effect, you can remove it by clicking the null icon in the upper right corner of the palette. Experiment with the bevel styles to decide which will work best for the button.

3

Español

Add the button text. Select the Type tool (T) from the toolbox and click inside the image area of the button. Enter your text. Use the pop-up menus on the Type options bar to change the font and size of the type.

4 ## Español

Change the text color. Click the color swatch on the Type options bar; then choose a color from the color picker. If the cube icon appears next to your color choice, you can click it to shift the color to the closest Web-safe color. This prevents browser dither when the color appears on a monitor that can display only 256 colors. Browser dither occurs when an 8-bit monitor attempts to display color that is in the image but not the color palette used by the browser. When you're satisfied with the color, click OK.

5 ## Español

Español

Reposition the text. If you want to move the text, reposition it using the the Move tool (✥). If you want to nudge the text in one-pixel increments, select the Move tool from the toolbox and use the arrow keys.

6 **Save working and optimized versions of the image.** Choose File > Save As, rename the file, and save a working version of the button. This saves the file in Photoshop format and leaves all of the layers intact.

Then choose File > Save for Web. In the Save for Web dialog box, choose GIF from the Settings pop-up menu. When optimizing an image for the Web, it's always best to keep the file size as small as possible. To check the file size, look below the optimized preview of the button. Experiment with the use of fewer colors, using the Settings pop-up menu, to achieve a smaller size while retaining the image quality.

For design tips and information on using buttons in a navigation bar, see Project 19.

Variation: Create rollover button states

Use different layer styles to create two states for JavaScript rollovers, in which the appearance of a button changes when the user clicks or moves the pointer over the button.

1 **Copy the texture layer.** If the Layers palette is not visible, click the Layers tab in the palette well. Select the background layer and drag it over the Create a New a Layer icon (▣) to make a copy. Select the new layer. This layer will be the rollover state. Click the Layer Styles tab in the palette well. This time, select Inner Glows from the pop-up menu. Experiment with different effects. Also experiment with Inner Shadows and Image Effects.

2 **Save the changes to the working file.** Choose File > Save to save the file with the new state.

The file now contains two background layers: one with the bevel effect and one with another effect of your choice that reflects the rollover state change.

3 **Save a Web version of the rollover states.** Choose File > Save for Web. Follow the same procedure as given in step 6, except this time save the file with a name that indicates that it contains a rollover button.

After you have the two button states, you can create the JavaScript for the rollover button in a Web page layout program.

Use bold sans-serif fonts for the button text so it's easier to read on the screen.

COLOR!
Color coding your buttons can make Web site easier to navigate.

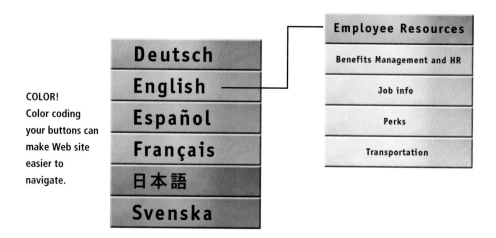

GOOD
A bold-faced font is good, but contrasting colors also increase legibility.

SIMPLE
Use simple photos or textures that don't interfere with the content on the button.

NOT GOOD
Light or serif fonts with minimal contrast can be difficult to read.

Project 19

Create a Navigation Bar
for the Web

Create a navigation bar to link destinations on your Web site.

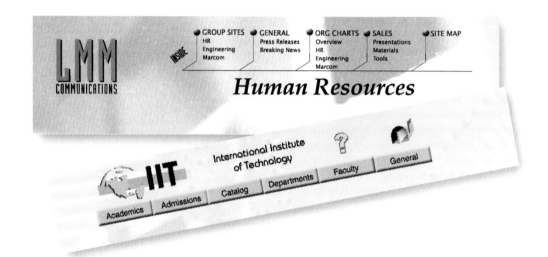

Navigation bars on a Web site help visitors find information quickly and stay oriented within the site. You can use the same navigation bar on every page on a site, or you can employ multiple navigation bars that use a button highlight to indicate the location for the viewer.

In this project, you create a horizontal or vertical navigation bar with your organization logo or other information of your choice by customizing a Photoshop Elements template. After creating the navigation bar, you will save an optimized version for the Web.

P19a.psd

P19b.psd

P19c.psd

P19d.psd

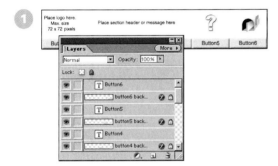

Get started. Open one of the template files for a horizontal or vertical navigation bar in the Proj19 folder.

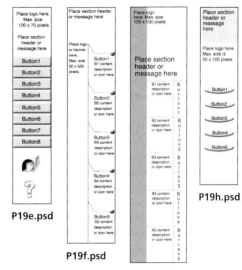

P19e.psd

P19f.psd

P19g.psd

P19h.psd

If the Layers palette is not visible, click the Layers tab in the palette well. All of the templates have several layers on the Layers palette. Any of the edits to the template will be done on these individual layers.

Bring in your logo. Open your logo file or other art file that you want to place in Photoshop Elements. Arrange the logo window next to the navigation bar window so that you can see both images. Using the Move tool (▸⊹) from the toolbox, drag the logo file into the navigation bar template. Position it according to the template; then click the eye icon for the Place Your Logo layer to hide the layer.

Add your company message.
Double-click the Place Section Header or Message Here layer on the Layers palette. Replace the selected text with your company name or a message. Change the font and size by using the pop-up menus on the options bar. If you want to change the font color, click the color swatch on the options bar and select a new color using the color picker.

Note: The Type tool(**T**) must be selected for the type options to appear.

If you don't want to add a company name or a message, click the layer's eye icon to hide the layer.

Enter your button text. On the Layers palette, double-click the Button 1 layer. Replace the selected text with your button text. Adjust the size, font, and color of the text using the Type options bar as in step 3.

Repeat this step for the other buttons.

Change the background colors.
Most likely, you will want to change the background colors of the navigation bar and the buttons. Select the navigation bar's background layer on the Layers palette. (Some of the templates have two background layers, for gray and white areas.) Click the Default Color icon(▪) and select a color using the color picker. To ensure consistency and no dithering, click the Only Web Colors check box. After you have selected a color, click the background area of the image with the Paint Bucket tool (◇). Repeat for any button layers you want to change.

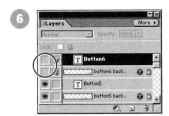

Hide any unused buttons. Click the eye icon to hide any unused button's text and background layers on the Layers palette. The button text and its background layer are linked, so you can easily rearrange the remaining buttons on the navigation bar. If you need to resize a button, first unlink the button background from the text so you don't distort the text. Then select the Move tool in the toolbox. Drag a handle to resize the button background. To resize a button more precisely, choose Image > Transform > Free Transform and enter height and width values on the options bar

Some of the templates have a question mark icon and mailbox icon. Hide these layers if you don't want to use them.

7 **Save a working file.** Choose File > Save As, rename the file, and save a working version of the navigation bar. This saves the file in Photoshop format and keeps all of the layers intact in case you want to make changes.

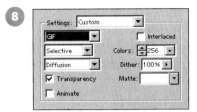

Save for the Web. Choose File > Save for Web. In the Save for Web dialog box, choose GIF from the Settings Pop-up menu. When optimizing an image for the Web, it's always best to keep the file size to a minimum. To check the file size, look below the optimized preview of the button. To achieve a smaller size while retaining the image quality, experiment with fewer colors using the Settings pop-up menu.

Variation: Create highlighted buttons

This technique allows you to create navigation buttons with a highlight— good for showing the locations within a Web site. Each version of the navigation bar that contains a different highlighted button will need to be saved separately. When the Web pages are created, these separate versions will be used for their designated pages.

1 **Copy the button text layers.** Select the button text layer and drag the layer over the New Layer icon (🗊) on the Layers palette. Double-click the new layer name on the Layers palette to change the name. Type the word *highlight* next to the name of the layer.

Create the highlight. Make sure that your new text highlight layer is selected; then double-click to select the text. Click the color swatch on the options bar and choose a highlight color in the color picker.

There are now two versions of each button text layer: one with the original color and one with the highlight color.

Repeat steps 1 and 2 for the remaining buttons to which you want to apply a highlight.

③ Set up the visible layers for the first button. Click the eye icon to hide the original button text layer of the first button. Make sure that the eye icon is visible for the highlighted text layer. The other buttons should have their highlighted text hidden.

④ Export the first navigation bar. Choose File > Save for Web. Save the file with the same settings as for the original navigation bar.

⑤ Export the remaining navigation bars. Repeat steps 3 and 4 for each highlighted button that you created.

Before you design a navigational system for your Web site, you should have a clear idea of where your readers will need to go. Create a flowchart of your site that clearly shows each location and how it will be accessed. A good rule of thumb is to have all main links accessible from the interior pages.

MAP IT OUT
Map your site so you know its navigation needs.

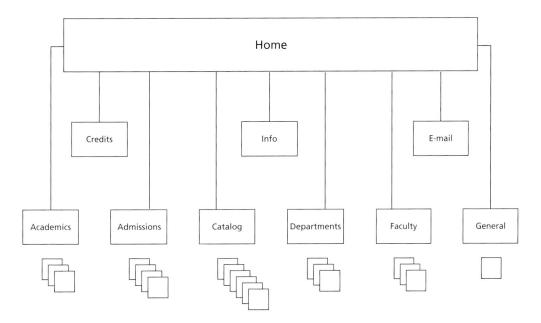

Index

Production Notes

This book was created electronically using Adobe FrameMaker®. Art was produced using Adobe Illustrator, Adobe Photoshop Elements, Adobe Photoshop, and Adobe PageMaker. The Cochin and Frutiger families of typefaces are used throughout this book.

Photography Credits

EyeWire, Inc.
Getting Photos Ready (*boy, business man, young woman, skier, person with kayak, young couple, cyclist, skater*); Project 7 (*business man and woman, surfer*); Project 12 (*calculator, woman on phone*); Project 13 (*farm fields, microscope, windmills, violinist*); Project 11 (*exercise woman, aerobics*); Project 16 (*skiers*); Project 17 (*globe, hands*)

Adobe Studio
Project 1 (*posing man in suit*)

Elizabeth Pham
Project 11 (*wedding photo*)

Julieanne Kost
Project 1 (*sky background*); Project 2 (*couch, chair, pumpkins*); Project 4 (*all photos*);

Lisa Matthews
Project 5 *(all photos); Project 6 (all photos); Project 8 (all photos); Project 9 (sunflower)); Project 10 (all photos); Project 14 (greek island)*

Photodisc, Inc.
Project 2 *(windmill)*; Project 12 *(test tubes, dam, wheat)*;